A Bowl of Pho and a Rainbow Serpent

My Cultural Life Journey and the
Footprints I Leave Behind

Terry Donnelly

A Bowl of Pho and a Rainbow Serpent
My Cultural Life Journey and the Footprints
I Leave Behind

First published in Australia by Terry Donnelly 2023

A catalogue record for this
book is available from the
National Library of Australia

ISBN: 978-0-646-88742-5 (pbk)

Typesetting and design by Publicious Book Publishing
Published with the assistance of Publicious Book Publishing
www.publicious.com.au

Book cover image: © singh_lens (shutterstock)

Contents

Foreword

On my first trip to Vietnam in 2016 I was a student halfway through an international relations degree. I was young and eager to get stuck into creating worldwide change and tackling the myriad of issues we faced across the globe. At the time, I was travelling to Vietnam for a job through which I hoped to learn as much as I could about changemaking in different parts of the world. And this trip did not disappoint – in fact it changed my life. But not in the way I had imagined.

When I met Terry Donnelly, I spent two weeks staying in his home and learning about his work.

It was there I began to notice what I now refer to as the *ripple effect*.

Terry works with a centre for children with disabilities in rural Vietnam. Over many years, and through a thousand small steps, Terry has worked to support the wellbeing of not only the children in the centre, but that of the entire community surrounding it. While Terry dedicated his own energy and resources to this place, he also made it possible for others to do the same. Terry found ways to employ locals in need of work at the centre. He connected young students from around the world with this opportunity to see grassroots community change firsthand. He made it possible for a loving and vibrant international community to connect through their love for this one small corner of the world, and the people who live there.

When Terry began this work however, he did not anticipate the vast ripple effect he would have. He did not set out to create worldwide change, he simply created space for it to grow. When I first met Terry, he loaned me a book. While walking me to my taxi to the airport at the end of my visit he said, "Take this book, read it if you like, but make sure you bring it back to me as I am very fond of it." That is how I ended up in Terry's world. He made space for me to become part of his community and because of that, I ended up returning to Vietnam six times over the past few years.

During this time, I have completed studies in both international relations and a masters in positive psychology. I have made it my life's work to guide young people to be agents for positive change where they are, using the resources they have available to them. I run a not-for-profit in Australia which teaches young people to create positive change in their own lives, and in the world around them. Over the past six years, our organisation has helped hundreds of young people to take action about something that matters to them – where they are, with what they have.

I felt honoured to be asked to write a foreword for this book. I have always had a love for the kind of person who sees something wrong in the world, and decides to do something about it. When I met Terry Donnelly I thought, 'Here is someone who is doing exactly that'.

Terry has had a profound impact on my life and I have carried his story of bravery, openness and deep care with me through my work and my life since meeting him. Terry taught me that we can do something good, wherever we are. We do not need to wait for the opportunity, or to be asked: good things happen when we decide to make them happen.

Terry's story shows us how one person's actions in one small community can have ripples of change around the world. To me, this begs the question – what if every one of us decided to do one thing – just one thing – to create a change where we are? How far could your ripple spread?

The last few years have challenged us all in different ways. Terry's story of overcoming challenges by embracing the sad, the scary, the uncertain and the unexpected, may be just the story we all need to bravely take action – to do something good.

My hope for this book is that it inspires you to start your one good thing, whatever that may be.

Avalon Bourne
Program Director at Sonder Youth

There is melancholy in the wind and sorrow in the grass
Charles Kuralt

Melancholic people dream of perfection and
they are disappointed when they realize they cannot
achieve that state, or ideal Don't be afraid
of the blue, understand it
Zet

Introduction

A strange way to start a book but it is relevant as I have had times like that in my life in that state—searching, hoping to find that ideal space that I was meant to occupy, that beautiful place where everything and everybody is exactly as you would like it to be. That place that has green pastures, shade trees, flowers, a river running through it or a view of the ocean, animals running freely and people who only have one mission in life: to be happy and to share that happiness and peace with others.

An ideal state but for the vast majority of us it is not and will not be realised, so our mission is to find that happiness in the life that we do have, to realise that you are who you are meant to be and that you exist where you are meant to exist. To find true happiness always seemed challenging to me as it appeared that there was forever something missing. Although the journey has been long and the wisdom needed was difficult to attain, that goal is now near. Everything I ever wanted was always close by, within; I just didn't know where to look or how to attain it as I was focused on my material needs while ignoring my spiritual needs. True happiness lives within and we just need to know how to release it on a permanent basis.

Do I now have that pretty, scenic picture painted above? No, but maybe one day I will stumble across it or it will find me.

Do I now have true happiness and peace in my life? If I am to be brutally honest, not yet, I still occasionally feel those frustrations build in my body when things are not as I think they should be or when people's actions are contrary to my beliefs. Those frustrations could easily turn into anger, hatred, confusion and many other negative emotions. For me, they do not—I now control my emotions, they do not control me.

Am I close to attaining that true happiness and peace in my life? Yes, I believe so. It has been a long journey to this day and many choices have been made—none wrong, none right, but each a lesson of its own.

I have shared moments in my life with the blue and, for a short period of time, the black. It was during that black time that I found myself in a state of despair and true hopelessness, wondering how it came to be and if I would ever surface from it. All through that time I wondered if there was an easier way. For many, the alternatives are suicide, alcohol or drug addiction; for others, some form of therapy, searching for something to take away the pain. For me, it was just one word: why?

Once I understood the why, it wasn't so daunting; once I truly understood then I knew I could claw my way back out. When I did understand, life itself became clearer to me: the type of person I wanted to be and the type of life I wanted to live was much more attainable.

The blackness passed but the blue returns in rare fleeting moments and I am comfortable with that for I am human, and sadness at times comes to us all. For me, it is now a feeling of peace mixed with a tinge of sadness—tears still fall at moments when you least expect it to happen, but now each time they do, I know what must be done and soon they disappear again. The reason I believe that most people suffer depression and slip into the deep black hole is that they are not willing to face the realities of life and their own circumstances, which often arise from the choices they have made. The black is an easy place to go if you want to escape reality, if you don't want to make the decisions you need to make, and if you do not accept the life you have created. To climb back, you need the willpower and belief to do so and to acknowledge why you are there in the first place. Most who don't recover lack the belief in themselves to move forward or are just not comfortable with what that may bring.

I want to give a brief insight into life for me as it has been and as it may be from time to time in the future, as I continue to work towards true peace and happiness. The road ahead will be paved by me, the potholes will be created by me and the roadblocks again my creation, but now I know I can overcome them. I have responsibility first to myself, for if I can't function then those around me also suffer. Secondly, I have a huge responsibility to the many people who share my life and to the delicate and sensitive work that my international family and I are involved in.

So, I will wear the blue when I need to and thank it for making me aware that all is not as it should be. When a tear falls, morning, afternoon or as I lay at night, I will question it and arrive at the answer in my own unique way. All of that searching for who I really am and what purpose I have in this life, I have long left behind. I am Terry Donnelly and what will become of me will unfold in due time. For now, I will be content and accept each moment as it arrives, living in the knowledge that I have the capacity to overcome anything that lies ahead and that my choices, *only* my choices, will define who I am and what I will do in these remaining years.

Each day I live by the four basic tenets below and in good conduct.

Love, Compassion, Understanding, Truth

Sometimes I will stray, for I am only human, but each day I vow to stray less.

A Little Bundle of Joy

During my life to date I have been lucky enough to have many beautiful children enter my life and show me what true resilience is and how to give joy to others by just being yourself. Today I met another of those sweet souls, Nu, a very young child from a remote Hmong village in the mountainous area of Son La province, Northern Vietnam.

Nu suffered third degree burns to sixty per cent of her body and spent three months in the burns unit of a hospital in Hanoi. She now has to constantly make the seven-hour bus trip to Hanoi for ongoing treatment. A good friend and charity colleague of mine, An Phan, introduced Nu to me and now she and her parents will spend time with me at my house when they come to town.

No matter what you give, it will never be equal to how much you receive. Last night we sat, attempted communication, smiled and laughed a lot. For a time nothing else mattered, she had a new friend and I had a heart full of joy. I sometimes wonder if these little ones with so much poverty and pain in their lives know of the joy they give you, of the motivation they give to make you want to do more, of the many reasons they give you to never feel self-pity, and the understanding they give you that the material world has little meaning without love in it. Your gift to them is love and caring; their gift to you is immeasurable.

Having lived and worked in Vietnam for twelve years I have been blessed to meet many children in similar situations to Nu. The wording of that sentence may seem a little strange—it could have read *I have been saddened to meet…*. That may be true in some part but they would not want me to feel sadness, for you then relay

1

that to them; all they really want is friendship and the knowledge that somebody loves and cares for them. Most people I have found here in Vietnam in similar circumstances to Nu's family don't really understand what they are 'missing out' on. They only know the life they have and no matter how poor or how difficult their life is they are still so willing to share. They may not have the material means to share but I have rarely met more generous, giving and happy people, especially when you consider their circumstances. They aren't really missing out on anything; they already have what others seek: love and happiness.

I founded and ran the Red Lotus Foundation (RLF), a volunteer service in Vietnam, and also Helping Hands Vietnam (HHV), an informal charity. We focus primarily on one disability centre in Ba Vi province and one in Bac Ninh province.

The Thuy An Disability Centre in Ba Vi, which is a government-run facility is approximately sixty kilometres away from the Vietnamese capital of Hanoi. I walked through the gates of the centre ten years ago with my coordinator and dear friend Hanh. It was very confronting and I felt like I had entered another world—not even a third world, it went beyond that. It was like a sad movie that you hope will soon finish with a happy ending and you will it to do so, but that ending has not arrived yet; it is something we work towards each day with help from the centre staff. If you named each physical and intellectual disability that has been documented I am sure it would be found here. I didn't realise what a huge part this particular place would play in my life, as that day I just felt empty. I left with tears in my eyes but also felt gratified, knowing that we would have an opportunity to help these beautiful children.

I credit this place for my personal education in the true meaning of compassion and it has grounded me completely; it has taught me how to love unconditionally and to give without seeking reward. It has taught me the deeper meaning of understanding and to be true to myself and others, and that I also have the capacity to help create an environment to help and advance others in need. It is said that we have no obligation in life to help anybody other than ourselves; that may be true for some, but those words ring empty to me.

To effect change, change the way you see things
Zet

Early on in our work in Ba Vi we really needed assistance from a larger number of volunteers, but now as our Helping Hands team has grown we only accept returning volunteers and their families, friends or referrals from them. We bring just enough volunteers to assist our local HHV workers with their duties and are happy to have those with previous experience here. Our work is very sensitive and our workplace very emotional; it is not suitable for everyone.

I also personally work at another centre called Huong La, in Bac Ninh province. We have not placed volunteers there, I just go out each week for a couple of days and find funds when I can to contribute to a food budget for the kids and bring some much-needed equipment for the physically disabled to participate in the programs I am setting up. The centre is run by a group of nuns, the Sisters of Unity; they are unlike any people I know—their days are full of caring for the children, working and praying. They grow their own vegetables and fruit to eat, catch fish in their small dam, work tirelessly in the fields, do construction at the centre, make candles for income and they inspire me simply by being the wonderful human beings that they are.

At night, when I stay out at the centre in this very small village, I feel nothing but peace and total admiration for the sisters and the work they do. I am more Buddhist than Christian in my beliefs but that does not matter to them as we have one common goal and primary purpose—to enhance the lives of the children we care for. I respect their religion and practices as I do Buddhist teachings and any other religion. All religions and teaching have as their core values *Love, Compassion, Understanding and Truth*: the four basic tenets we should all live by to find a life that is truly dominated by happiness.

My journey has been much more than the now. It has also been about loss of identity, reconnection, confusion to clarity—struggles that define us when we overcome them—and finding my way. I have learned much from many; I have explored religions, cultures and teachings, but in the end there is my way and there is your way. I am not a clone and neither are you; write your own book, that is, create your own pathway using what works for you.

Beginnings

I'm getting a little too far ahead of myself and have a few other things to talk about, so I guess I should start right at the beginning. I was born in a small country town called Gunnedah, located in the north-west of New South Wales, Australia. Nothing remarkable about my entry into the world and nothing really remarkable occurred on that day elsewhere. The front page news included: *Manly buses stop again; Queen asked not to visit Western Australia due to a polio epidemic; Waterfront timber shed fire; Arabs blamed for bus ambush* and *Sydney University expands research work into animal husbandry,* and Tony Bennett was Number One on the Billboard charts with *There'll Be No Teardrops Tonight*. I had a small mention in the births and deaths notices of the local paper.

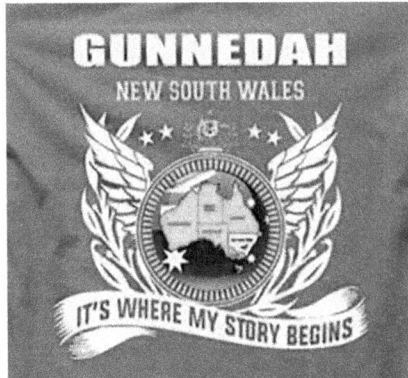

Brothers – Brian, Phillip, Greg, Garry

Mum and Dad

Mum

Early Days

Dad preparing to
serve in World War 2

The first breath as we leave the comfort of our mother's womb, a gasp, then a helping hand and we enter this world, little knowing at the time that we are entering to one day take our last breath and the time in between is as yet undetermined. For some a short period of time, for others it may at times seem too long, and again for others they will feel blessed to have lived for such a long period of time in relative happiness.

I have had the misfortune of seeing far too many babies and children pass from this life due to diseases that could have been treated in my home country, and tiny lives lost that could have been saved in a different time and space.

As a child and a young person we at times do not have any control over our immediate destiny as that environment is largely created by those entrusted with our care: mothers, fathers, relatives, teachers, carers, and others who will have some influence in the type of being we are in our infant years, and the type of being we are destined to become as a young adult. Later in life we will make our own choices and must be willing to accept the consequences of our actions and the chance to learn from life's lessons. When we have the right to make our own decisions there is no one to blame but ourselves; to dwell and blame our current circumstances on the past and to place blame on others for things that are occurring now will only hinder growth—best to let it go.

Inevitably, we will have the opportunity to decide the quality of the life that we are given and, for some, the choice of when it will end.

I was the second of five boys and a sister who we lost prior to birth due to some medical complications. Life was not easy but nowhere near as difficult as many others in the world faced at that time and still do today, maybe now in even greater measure. When I think back to my youth, there was a certain innocence about the world as a whole, very much unlike today where modern technology and the seemingly endless persecution of certain religions, ethnicities, races and political ideologies all now make this world, to me, a very scary place.

My childhood was not as ideal as I would have liked but I am not about to write a sad story about my youth and other moments throughout my life—I don't seek sympathy and I don't dwell in the past. I have felt my father's belt wrap around my legs, the switch across my butt, his big hands coming down hard on me and, on one occasion a little later, his fist; some of those things seemed to be the norm back in those days. On reflection, there are things that occurred which have shaped who I am today and it is not my intention to cast aspersions on others, some who have passed and some who are still with us. What happened, happened; there are things I have released and my mind is firmly in the now, I am at peace with my past.

I think my family was quite poor, or maybe it was just the times we lived in, but I do recall us eating many different varieties of animal offal—stomachs, hearts, livers, kidneys and tongues. I never want to look at another bowl of tripe (stomach lining of sheep or cattle) again as it seemed to be a regular meal during my childhood. Most of our meals tasted great no matter the source and I especially loved my mum's stuffed bullock heart; in times of need it is amazing what you can make a feast out of. We used to go to the edge of town, to the hillsides and plains to trap rabbits and we also used to spotlight them at night. We would drive around a paddock in the back of a utility with a spotlight attached to a battery and when you placed the spotlight on a rabbit it would be transfixed and not move until someone on foot was very close by. Then the usually short chase would be on, until the rabbit was caught or we lost another meal.

We raised our own chickens for their eggs and meat, we had a large vegetable garden and some fruit trees—I still yearn for Mum's mulberry pies cooked in the wood oven. We would also fish a lot and catch craybobs, which are also known as yabbies or freshwater crayfish; they were considered something of a delicacy. It's quite ironic to look back and to realise the way that we lived is the way that a lot of people nowadays are seeking. A simple life that relied on self-sufficiency; no frozen foods, takeaways or supermarket specials, it was just a good healthy lifestyle which brought with it a lot of happiness in the process. Every Sunday we sat down to a family roast; everybody had to be there, no excuses. We usually didn't need any as it was a meal that most families looked forward to back then, no mobile phones, no distractions, just a time for family to be together to enjoy a meal and talk about events in our lives.

From my childhood I also retain two of the happiest days I can remember as a family. The first was one particular day when we all went fishing at the local river. We set up in different locations and I sat close by my mum on an old tree trunk that stretched out over the river. We only needed to drop our line down beside the trunk and that day we had an endless supply of fish as they just seemed to come one after the other. I am not sure how many were caught that day but we ate fish for quite a long time after that.

The other day was the day it snowed in Gunnedah. Our town was very hot in the summer and very cold in the winter with numerous early morning frosts but it had never snowed and nobody would expect it to, given our location. One day it was particularly cold and although it may have only been frozen rain (sleet), for us it will always be the day it snowed in Gunnedah. Our next door neighbours were the Jones family and at that time they were building a new house and had just laid all the floor boards. The snow settled very nicely on that area and both families were out there playing in the wet and throwing snowballs (or sleet balls) at each other; we would run to various other parts of our property having these snowball wars. After a couple of hours of this we were all wet and freezing so it was inside for a warm shower, a change of clothes and then we gathered around the open fire. Mum brought over some bread and we used our three-pronged toasting fork to toast the bread over the open fire. We added strawberry or blueberry jam with a liberal dose of whipped cream, and along with a cup of tea we had the perfect snack for a cold winter's day.

My memories of the fishing day, the day it snowed and of course the Sunday roast lunches were all very simple and innocent times, a time for family, a time to really share what was important in life: love and happiness. I would of course have many memories, some I care to relate and others I choose not to, because to me, even back then, what was important was caring and sharing—sometimes it happened, sometimes we yearned for it.

On a cold winters night
There is nothing like the warmth of family
Zet

I have lived in Vietnam for the past twelve years and although I was never as poor as many here, I can relate a little to their circumstances and empathise with them. I have met so many with so little who are still willing to share what they have. They find happiness in the simplest of things and in their customs. The Buddhist philosophy has a lot to do with people's mindsets, for if you are born into a poor or difficult lifestyle, you should live your life well and in good conduct, for in the next life you will be rewarded with a higher station.

You cannot miss what you have never experienced
To yearn for something out of reach will usually
just bring heartache
Zet

Over the years my mother and father had a variety of occupations and always made sure we had three full meals a day and were clothed appropriately. I cannot imagine how difficult it must have been to raise five boys in those times but they did, and although none of us are perfect we are reasonably good beings and have raised families of our own. I don't recall a great deal about my brothers' childhoods even though we grew up together in the same house as we all seemed to float in different circles. Also, at that time my mind was always a little preoccupied with something I was too young to be thinking about—my future.

We are all now the best of friends and share a common love and bond that is sometimes difficult to embrace when younger as we were all at that time influenced by different friendship groups. Although we had our battles in the house, as would be expected with five boys, I also knew that if there was any external trouble the people I could count on most would be my brothers.

Gunnedah was a small country town of around 10,000 people and is still much the same today. I was happy there but in my mind it was not somewhere I would be for too long. Like most others in town I was heavily involved in sports and at five years old joined the local swimming club, remaining there for ten years. It was tiring, with training sessions early morning and every afternoon. I dreaded being woken at 6 am at the start of the season when there was still a chill in the air and having to dive into that freezing outdoor pool to do endless laps. Many a day I just clung to the wall at the end of the pool until Eric, our coach, would kick me out of the squad and tell me to go home. I would come back in the afternoon and he would let me rejoin. This was an annual event between us; he was a good man and taught me a lot, not only about swimming but also discipline and courage.

I played and competed in a variety of other sports. My father and his brothers were well-known rugby league players, a road that I would later also follow.

RAY, ROCKY AND REG DONNELLY, *three bothers of the famous footballing family who are expected to be at the big league re-*

**My father Reg on the right, with his brothers Ray and Rocky.
The start of the Donnelly football tradition.**

In those times, the good thing about sports is that they would take you out of town to compete in carnivals which gave the opportunity to be billeted out with families from other towns. I recall going to a state swimming carnival in Sydney as a small country boy and I was billeted with some lads from the inner city. The city scared me and so did they, they would jump on the back of buses in the middle of the city and ride for a few blocks before the conductor spotted them and kicked them off; or they would go into a clothing store and steal clothes by placing them under the clothes they wore. They also stole money in games rooms and would then run off with staff in hot pursuit. They were always running from somebody and I just tried to keep up, along with my cousin John, who was usually billeted with me on these trips.

They also showed us a glimpse into a world that was completely unknown to us at the time—girls. Sure, we had girls in Gunnedah but as yet had not really discovered the connection. City boys and girls were certainly very different and more advanced in many ways than their country cousins.

GUNNEDAH SCHOOL BOY'S RUGBY LEAGUE BOGGABRI
Third from the front

The little lad—Junior Swim Champion

We were a pretty unruly group of kids and the night before each out-of-town school rugby league carnival we would gather in groups and go around the neighbourhood raiding the orange and mandarin trees for our half-time refreshments during the games. Thinking back, I am sure most of the people in town knew this was going to happen and allowed it to slip by, as did the teachers/coaches, as we always left a bag full of bounty on the front porches of their houses. I remember Carey 'Para' Smith yelling to us one night that he found a tree of monster oranges so we all ran there with much excitement only to find him coming back over the fence with a bag full of grapefruit; he lived with that mistake for some years. On sporting trips the bus would always stop at a town for lunch or a toilet break and we boys would break off and find a souvenir-type shop or general store and while some kept the staff busy we would fill our pockets with all sorts of sweets and goodies.

My friends and I seemed to fixate on pinching things and were always up to something. Like the time my parents signed me up to the local Scout group, I guess in the forlorn hope that I may learn a little discipline; unfortunately this didn't work either. One night after our weekly Scout group meeting a couple of other boys and I decided we would raid the storage area of a local supermarket.

We knew there were bottles of cordial stored near the back gate, and as it was summer and we were thirsty we thought it a good idea at the time. We didn't steal things for monetary gain—I guess our escapades came from being bored in a small country town and what we took we did just to satisfy either our thirst or hunger. Unfortunately, on this occasion we were caught by the security guard and then handed over to the police. Yep, we were bad boys, but not *bad* bad boys. As we would say, it was all a bit of a lark. My time with the Scouts came to an abrupt halt, without one leadership badge to my name.

Leadership is something I would learn about a little later in life and is something I have embraced in certain roles throughout my life; always in an inclusive manner, not in a dictatorial way. That is not leadership at all, it's just fuel for somebody's ego.

I spent most of my youth on weekends and during holidays—when I wasn't involved in sport—at my grandmother, Florence's house. She was my protector, my safe haven and it was as though when I was with her nothing could touch me. There was just Grandma and me, and although it may seem a little selfish I was happy with that. During the day I would run errands and go to the local shop to buy food for Grandma to cook or I would just play out in the yard. Each night we would hop into the big double bed and Grandma would take her Bex powder then off to that peaceful sleep we would go. Life was simple with Grandma, some of the happiest days of my life; she is never far from my mind and in times of need I still seek her counsel in meditation.

Time passed and Grandma started to suffer ill health as she aged. One night my mum had her stay at our house as she was really concerned about her wellbeing. Grandma slept in the bed opposite me and during the night I heard a thud and woke to see her lying on the floor; she had rolled out of bed and was in a great deal of distress. She was taken to hospital and diagnosed with a broken hip. I visited her on one occasion but was too saddened to return again as I could not bear to see her that way. Little did I know that it would be the last time I would see her—or did I know? I think I may have been around twelve or thirteen years old at the time and although I knew something about death, of course, I never thought that I would be this close to it. One day I came home from school and my mother told me that Grandma had passed away. I acknowledged it but immediately put it to the back of my mind as it was something I did not want to believe and didn't understand. So life went on as normal for me; in my mind Gran was still with me.

A few days later we attended the funeral, my first. The family walked in to church and headed to the front and as we got closer I noticed the coffin and realised that my grandma was in there. Right at that moment my mother started to cry uncontrollably; that is when my dam also burst and for the first time I knew that no matter how much I tried to deny it or not believe it, it was true. My grandma had left me for good. I just thought, why? What would I do now?

Yes, I would miss her and all of the good times we shared but I was also scared, as Grandma provided a safe haven for me; a place and a person to be with to find my true happiness and peace.

Later in life I would learn that the person I loved and cherished so much was not my grandmother but in reality my great-grandmother. There was much to learn about who I was and invaluable lessons to come about the occupation of this country and the consequences it had and still has for the original inhabitants of this land, the Aboriginal people. I would be enlightened but also confused by the revelations that awaited me, but that is a little further down the track, not for now.

Death will always unsettle you, people precious to you will one day leave you, or you them; the length of time we have is the only thing in this life that is truly uncertain. In Vietnam they say you should not cry for the dead. Of course there will be tears shed in the first instance but what that saying means is do not mourn endlessly for someone who has passed, else their spirit will not be released and they cannot move on. One thing you cannot change in life is death and it is bad enough that one person should lose their life, so there is no reason for another to stop living in the now because of that; endless mourning changes nothing, it

15

only brings sadness to those that do it. Yet there are some who embrace that mourning and will sometimes use it as an excuse for other aspects of their life. There is little room in this life for 'if only'.

**Live each day as though death awaits you in sleep this night
Your last meeting is how people will remember you
If you are kind and caring and you don't stray from the path
Their thoughts will always be good**

Zet

Two years after Grandma's passing, it was time to make the first independent choice of my life and to take the first tentative steps that would lead me down the path to where I am today.

At the time of writing I am living in an apartment in the Ha Dong district, Hanoi, Vietnam. I am just writing some words on a laptop, not sure why, just knowing it should be done and from this something will evolve. Sometimes in life you are just given a direction and you can choose to follow it, or not—this is one of those moments. Do I have something to contribute? I don't know, the words are only my thoughts and knowledge gained from my life experience. I have created a way of life that brings me peace, comfort and love, so I hope that some of these words help others along their way. It might not contain good grammar or sentence structure for it is written by me and my words should fall the way they do. I am not a writer, just someone with a story to tell in my own way.

I also hope these words will reach my grandchildren, of which I currently have six, Eli, Nate, Blakely, Ahlei, Daphne Heather and Peter. I don't recall my grandfather on my father's side and have never spoken of him, nor has anyone else to me. I am unsure why that is—I don't imagine there are any dark secrets but perhaps some things that have been left unspoken. I do know of my grandfather on my mother's side, but would never meet him because of a family secret, one that would impact me greatly. I hope by this writing, my grandchildren will have an account of the type of person their grandfather was and I also hope it will impact them in a positive manner.

Choices

The first choice I made that would greatly affect my current life was that I decided I didn't need any further education. Later in life I would return for a short time to formal education as a part-time college student but for now, life was to be my teacher.

I would make mistakes along the way but that is the way of life; don't let failure destroy you, learn and grow from it. Failure is just another negative word that is used in various circumstances and it simply means the choices made or the pathway chosen was not right for you in that particular time and space. We should never feel the emotion that the word can invoke, rather we should learn from it, change direction and move on. If you don't get to the top of the mountain it doesn't mean you have failed, it just means that you reached your capacity at a certain level and your achievement to reach that level was remarkable. Not too many climb to the top and those that do may be left wondering if it was worthwhile. It isn't how far you go that's important; it's how you get there that is.

We make some of our children failures even before they leave school. We all have different capacities to achieve in different areas, in different ways. Our educational system compartmentalises young children by handing out test results marked 'F' which starts the process of giving that child an inferiority complex he or she would be much better without; this just hinders future learning, it does not enhance it. We should learn from the Nordic system where no official marks are given in primary school. The primary benchmark should be to pass in happiness because with that comes a willingness to learn.

The only thing I excelled at in school was sports. I spent a lot of time in the principal's office for bad behaviour and many a day I had swollen hands from those who chose to dispense punishment with a cane. I had one particular teacher who appeared to find a perverse joy in sending me to the principal and although I am sure there were times I had contributed to that, in my young mind it was always somebody else's fault. One day she boldly declared to the class that she would send four students to the headmaster before the end of class and about five minutes from time she had three, so she looked over at me and said, "Donnelly you'll do, off you all go."

I must admit that at times I did deserve to go, but not on that particular day. I also learned a valuable lesson at the vice-principal's office one day when he told me directly he was going to give me four cuts of the cane but before doing so he asked if I had anything wrong with my hands. Hoping to reduce the amount of cuts to two on one hand I told him I had injured the thumb on my left hand playing football. The result was four cuts on my right hand. The lesson: never lie.

I did have an occasion for six cuts of the cane, the maximum allowed at that time, when I was sent with two friends of mine, Carl 'Fats' Gardner and Wayne 'Bugs' Kellow, to the vice-principal's office. We had been waiting outside the office for a long time and were unsure if the vice-principal, Mr Rigby, was in the office or not, so we asked Bugs to have a look around the door. As he leaned over to glance inside, Fats and I gave him an almighty push, resulting in him falling to his hands and knees and sliding across the floor and under Mr Rigby's desk before finally coming to a halt with his head almost resting in Mr Rigby's lap. Peering downward between his legs, all that Mr Rigby could see was Bugs's head—needless to say the caning was given with some extra venom that day.

At the age of 15, I left school not knowing what I wanted to do or where I wanted to go. I have never had any regrets regarding that because although I may have appeared to be a complete rascal, I did know even at that age that something awaited me and there would be a purpose in my life. It turns out that like everyone, there is always more than one purpose.

While you are busily searching for your purpose in life
Life itself has passed you by

Zet

Work and Life in Sydney

My first venture into meaningful employment was as an apprentice tractor mechanic for Mr Frank O'Keefe, a good man, who was at that time also the mayor of our town. It was to be a short-lived tenure of around six months; it was heavy, dirty and hard work but that was not the reason for leaving. I was fifteen years old and working, earning $16 per week and discovering demons, one of which was alcohol. I was also enjoying the company of girls and partying. Although it was common for men to work each day then go to the pub for a few beers, it was not appropriate for a fifteen-year-old living at home with his parents. Still, I tried, but living with my parents was always doomed to fail. If I wanted to explore this lifestyle in complete freedom it would mean leaving home. Thus, I decided at fifteen years and six months of age that I would go to Sydney, that big scary place I had visited some years ago.

That small period of time of work and play was just a precursor to what was to follow as I stepped out into the world to discover new things, new places and myself. The farewell with my mother was one of the sadder moments in my life as it still is each time we meet and part again. Nowadays, this is infrequent but the bond of a mother can never be broken; although she hears from and sees me more irregularly than any of her other sons, I know that of all the people I have met in this lifetime she is the one who understands me the most and who is willing to endure my shortcomings. Nothing replaces love, and love only exists with understanding.

I am not a person who feels the need to make regular contact with those that I love. I like to think that they can feel what I have in my heart for them no matter the distance or the time and to know that will never vary. But that is my way, not necessarily the way of all that I share special bonds with as they have different needs and occasionally I need to acknowledge that. Sometime later, when I was living on the Central Coast of New South Wales and had fathered four children I received a letter from my mother with a gentle reminder. Inside the envelope was a passport size picture of her and on the back of the photo was written 'This is your mother, ring her'. That picture is still with me and the memory still brings a smile to my face. Others may not always share your way, they may have needs greater than yours; you may feel that your love is unconditional and does not need to be reinforced constantly but there are those that do need that assurance. The letter and photo reinforced that for me and although I am still a little reticent in this area, I do try.

Sydney, sex, drugs and rock and roll were the things that went through my mind on the trip to the big city. Sex was discovered on my sixteenth birthday. Drugs, fortunately, had no appeal to me after one occasion when a friend called Ron and I each took a pill of a drug called LSD (or acid, as it was also known) and it took me to a place I never wanted to visit again. As for marijuana, it didn't really move me and I didn't like things that controlled my mind. It would be another sixteen years before I admitted to myself that that is exactly what alcohol does, and with this realisation I would also free myself of that particular drug. As for the rock and roll, that came in abundance and I was lucky to see many great artists of my time in concert: Eagles, Bee Gees, Rolling Stones, Doobie Brothers, Tina Turner and, of course, many local bands at venues around the city. One vivid memory was seeing one of the world's greatest rock and roll bands, ACDC, on stage at the Gunnedah Town Hall just before the world claimed them. Paul White, who I lived with for a short time, also educated me on music as he was an accomplished singer and musician. His brother Phillip had a silken voice and would also play a small part, not personally, but through my admiration of his skills.

My older brother Brian and friend Paul 'Pearly' White had already moved to the city and I went to join them in their boarding house in the suburb of Marrickville. The house was the home of two of the most wonderful people I have met, Ma and Pa Farrell; yes, as the name suggests they were just like grandparents and like all good grandparents they could only tolerate so much and if you didn't abide by their rules, there were consequences.

At that time, with me being me, rules did not play a huge part in my life, so after just a short time I moved on again. Although we had many discussions regarding my behaviour over the six-month period I was with them and although I did try to amend it, I could not see that a lot would change with me in the near future. Because they were such wonderful people I chose to willingly go and burden them no more. I had not done anything majorly wrong (in my view) and no one particular thing instigated my leaving but they had strict rules about female visitors and the use of alcohol and at that time in my life I knew that was a test I could not pass. Tears were shed that day by both me and Ma—I know she knew that I loved her as she loved me. I was young and had many lessons to learn and that would take some time, which I knew should not be to their detriment. I am sure she also shed tears of worry about what lay ahead for me as I was only sixteen years old and living in a still unfamiliar environment.

I have always understood that if you are a guest in another's house treat them and other occupants with respect, abide by the way they choose to live their lives, or leave. If you are a guest in another's country abide by their traditions, their culture, and the way they choose to live their lives, or leave. We have no right to impose our beliefs or ideals on anybody unless they invite you to and are willing to accept your way freely.

In a broader sense I have never been able to understand the reason why Christian people over the centuries and still today believe they have the right to impose their religion on everybody on the planet as they ceaselessly try to replace some already long-established and wonderful teachings. We also have so many ill-informed and ignorant people going to foreign countries with no understanding of the culture and vainly— and sometimes aggressively—trying to change a way of life that has existed for thousands of years.

My first job after arriving in Sydney was in the laundry at the Australian Hotel, which at the time was one of the most luxurious hotels in Sydney. Although I was assigned to the laundry as a washer person I loved the limited opportunities I had to deliver the laundry to the guests of the hotel as they were always generous tippers and my salary was quite lowly. I would hold many positions over the ensuing years I spent in Sydney, from an apprentice ladies' hairdresser to a short venture into modelling, construction, bricklayer's labourer, bottle shop attendant and barman. During these years I also saw too many of my close friends die from drug overdoses and others die from alcohol consumption. I would learn to surf, learn the benefits of a gym, and to a small degree change my lifestyle as a direct result of the losses I suffered.

Wee Waa Revelations

At around eighteen years of age I made a short trip back to my hometown, possibly with the thought in my mind that I could return and live there again. That was not to be but this trip had its lessons. I first went with a friend of mine to a very small outback town called Wee Waa to try to earn some money cotton chipping. This involved walking between the rows of cotton with a hoe and chipping away the weeds from the plants, usually in around 40°C heat. It was so hot that we would walk forward for a period of time and then backward to spread the sunburn on exposed skin. We were paid according to how many rows we chipped in a given time period. It was not something I would recommend to anyone—chipping in the daylight hours and drinking at night. For a time living in a real frontier town with hard people who had hard lifestyles.

During my school years I had many Aboriginal friends and didn't really see them as being different in any way. I think at that time Gunnedah was like that, accepting of everyone and our house was always full of many friends, both Aboriginal and white so to me there was really no difference. Wee Waa opened my eyes to a different side of Australia and the manner in which Aboriginal people were treated and how they were spoken to, mostly with contempt. I saw Aboriginal men and women openly assaulted in public places and knew of women sexually assaulted in not so public places and with no proper recourse to lawful aid. People thrown into the back of police vans each night, then thrown into the local jailhouse. Deaths in custody were not uncommon in those days, especially in this place and many other locations like it throughout Australia. Alcohol abuse was rife among the local community as was petrol sniffing but nobody in any authority seemed to want to help to address these issues in a positive way.

Seven years prior to my time in Wee Waa the noted Aboriginal activist Charles Perkins led what was known as the Freedom Ride through North West New South Wales partly in reaction to what was happening in the United States to the African American people as well as the Aboriginal people of Australia. The ride involved students and teachers from the University of Sydney who were to survey Aboriginal living conditions. The group also challenged a ban on Aboriginal ex-servicemen not being able to enter ex-servicemen's clubs. In the town of Walgett, when the local Aboriginal soldiers returned from the war they were feted in the local RSL (Returned Soldiers League) club for one day and then barred from entering again. A special window was set up so that they could purchase drinks from outside the club but they were not allowed inside; this was the same throughout the country. The ride would also challenge bans on Aboriginal children being barred from the Moree and Kempsey swimming pools.

I remember competing in swimming carnivals at Moree as a child and seeing all of the Aboriginal kids and families in one little pool off to the side as we swam and had our meeting in the big pool. I thought at the time it was because the meeting was being held in the big pool that nobody was allowed in there on that day, but that was not the case; I didn't know what segregation was or that it existed in my country. It was 1962 before Aboriginal people were given the right to vote and another five years following a referendum until they were included in the census. I find it quite ironic, considering Australia was their country first and the people giving them the right to enjoy the freedoms of their own country were actually the invaders. Those so-called freedoms also had strings attached through a series of policies that the then-government hoped would see the whitening of Australia. From 1943 selected Aboriginal people could apply for exemption certificates. In return exempted individuals were required to relinquish their language, identity and ties to kin.

The intergeneralisation trauma caused by these rules still has devastating effects for many Aboriginal people today. .

Another 14 years further down the track these events would have a significant and very real impact on my life.

A sad reflection on the government's arrogance and their abuse of power.

NEW SOUTH WALES GOVERNMENT
ABORIGINES PROTECTION ACT, 1909-1943, SECTION 18c
[REGULATION 56]

CERTIFICATE OF EXEMPTION

From Provisions of the Act and Regulations

THIS IS TO CERTIFY that ....

.... Aborigine, aged............ years, residing at ....
(caste)
is a person who in the opinion of the Aborigines Welfare Board, ought no longer be subject
to the   provisions   of the Aborigines Protection Act and Regulations, or any of such
following provisions
provisions, and he/she is accordingly exempted from such provisions:—

Photograph of

Issued in compliance with the Resolution of the Aborigines Welfare Board and dated the ....
.... day of ...., 19.......
................................Chairman.
................................Member.
of the Aborigines Welfare Board.

Countersigned by
The Secretary.

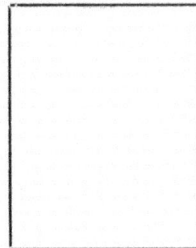

Signature of Holder ....

10029 2.63 V. C. N. Blight, Government Printer

Gunnedah Again

After my Wee Waa experience, I went back to Gunnedah but nothing had really changed. I was a couple of years older, had longer hair and thought that I had more rights than the fifteen-year-old who left town. That was not to be. My parents still had their rules that I was expected to abide by and the town was much the same as before; I was just that little older now and could legally enter hotels. Some visits turned into fights, always accompanied by a small degree of grief from my parents. This was a very small town and if you did something on a Friday night your parents knew about it by Saturday morning.

I can say with all honesty that I have never instigated a fight in my life as I didn't really see much point in solving things in that manner—I just seemed to have a head that others liked to hit. This has only happened on four occasions in my life, five if you count fighting one person twice in one night. There are times in life when confrontation cannot be avoided and when younger I found it hard to walk away. The results of the fights do not matter, each just the same, with the next day bringing an emptying feeling and inevitable questions as to why. None with any lasting hatred—you would meet up with your antagonist the next day, shake hands and go about life as before.

So, a couple of games of football, many late nights later and a haircut, courtesy of my father's counsel ('cut your hair or leave this house'), I headed back to Sydney. My only regret at the time was that I had cut my hair and decided to leave the next day anyway, minus my much-loved and cared-for locks. Still, external appearances are only a disguise; nothing can hide or alter the person you are.

During those days with my two best mates, Vernon 'Bluey' Bartlett (left)
a football legend back home and a great man we all looked up to;
Robert 'Changa' Jones (centre); yours truly (right); and John 'Dallas'
Donnelly (my cousin) (front).

Sydney Again, then Football and Surfboards

During this time in Sydney I met Linda, the first true love of my life. She was an English girl and although some years older than me, accepted me into her life and her family. She was a remarkable and caring person and we would spend almost five years together before parting. I can't really say why, it was just something that occurred mutually; maybe she tired of my partying ways and time spent away from her, living in different towns and cities to play football. I also needed to explore more of life, she was ready for marriage and children, I still had adventures in front of me.

The next couple of years did not see much change in my life in Sydney: work, surf, play and live life as it presented itself. The only real change was that I went back to playing rugby league, first with a local team my brother Brian played for and then in a competition sponsored by local business houses. It was here that my bond with Aboriginal people would be renewed as there was an all-Aboriginal team in the competition and I would find myself feeling more at home in their company than that of my own teammates. Some of the lads introduced me to the suburb of Redfern, the spiritual heartland for Aboriginal people in the city with an area affectionately known as The Block. I also had an introduction to La Perouse, another area of high cultural significance.

When I was twenty, I had a phone call from Micky Hicks, a friend of the family in my hometown of Gunnedah. Micky told me that he was to be the captain/coach of the local rugby league team in Byron Bay, a small town on the far north coast of New

South Wales and that he'd heard that I could play a bit. He asked if I would be interested in going there to play; they would find me accommodation, work and pay me to play. This immediately sparked an interest as Byron is renowned as a surfer's paradise and the fact that they were going to pay me to play football was at the time to me a bit of a hoot. Byron not only had some of the best surf breaks in Australia but was also well known for its hippie and alternative lifestyle, something I would cherish after my years spent in the city.

I spent a year in Byron alongside the locals, the surfers that migrated there, and the hippies that bought a wonderful alternative lifestyle to the town. At the time, Byron was no more than a big village and everyone in it seemed to support the local football team, making social occasions commonplace. This year turned out to be one of the happiest of my life.

I ended up living in a flat that overlooked the ocean and I could see two famous surf breaks from my balcony, Shipwreck and The Pass. I would rise in the morning and check the surf—if it was up, then surfing it would be. If it was a flat day, some friends and I would go out to the local abattoirs and hopefully get a day's casual work to earn a bit of money. Life was very simple. We would go fishing a lot, go prawning, buy cheap meat at the abattoirs for our protein, sometimes be given vegetables and with an abundance of local fruits and a winery nearby it seemed like heaven for a young twenty-year-old who wanted no more in life.

It was a wonderful year. We played a reasonable brand of football that saw us finish at mid-table, I surfed, partied and enjoyed being part of the community and its alternative lifestyle. On most nights you could go to a hotel and find footballers, locals, hippies and surfers all mingling as one and enjoying life in this little utopia. It is the one place I don't think I ever witnessed a pub fight—it was the era of love and peace, and this was the place to really experience that philosophy.

I was never a great surfer but loved the water and the challenges that each different wave presented. My favourite break was The Pass, where an accomplished surfer on the right day and with the right wave could ride it all the way onto Byron Beach itself. The surf breaks were ours on weekdays but on the weekend surfers and tourists would come from many different locations to test themselves in the surf or just to sample the unique lifestyle that was Byron.

It is a shame that these very waters that I loved so much would in eleven years' time take the life of someone I also loved very much: my cousin and one of my best friends, John 'Dallas' Donnelly.

John was nicknamed and referred to as Dallas because of his size—'bigger than Texas'—he was one of our gang of five in Gunnedah, a group of best mates who always hung out together when we were in Gunnedah at the same time and had the opportunity to do so. Our group comprised Kevin 'Shad' Moodie, Carey 'Para' Smith, Dallas and my brother from another mother, Robert 'Changa' Jones and of course me (then referred to as 'Tex'). We enjoyed each other's company and we enjoyed life to its fullest when together.

Dallas suffered from epilepsy since birth and had fits seemingly everywhere we went. I used to think he saved them up for me as he knew how much I disliked being around him when he had one. I thought he might find some perverse joy in my panic, such was his nature. Our relationship was one of mutual respect and love but if you had an opportunity to make a fool of the other, you took it. Dallas was a very accomplished and tough footballer and would represent at the highest level, playing for Australia. He was one of three footballers to do so from our small town (John O'Neill and Ron Turner were the others). I always thought that Dallas was of the mindset that his epilepsy would take him one day so he just lived life to the fullest and rarely took his prescribed medication on time.

One day when we were very young, we were training at the swimming club when I turned off the wall to see our coach Eric jumping into the water fully clothed and pulling Dallas out of the water. It was far from the first time I had seen Dallas have a fit but it was the first time I had seen it happen in the water; unfortunately it would not be the last time.

When we were around twenty years of age we had an occasion to be back home at the same time so we decided we would go out to Cushan's Reserve on the local Namoi River for a swim with my younger brother Phillip and a couple of local girls. We swam for a while then went to the mudslide on the other side of the river and began sliding from a reasonable height down the slide and into the river, before making our way back up the embankment and doing it all again. Dallas was walking up the slide at about the halfway mark when I noticed he was going to have a fit—usually when he was about to fit he would become unresponsive and get a totally blank look on his face. As the fit took control, he fell instantly onto the wet mud slide and slid down into the water. My brother Phillip and I looked at each other and immediately followed him in.

We told the girls to go to the other side of the river, where our clothes and cars were, and go to town for an ambulance as we continued to search for Dallas—no mobile phones back then. The river was a murky brown and the current was strong near the bank where Dallas went in; despite many attempts of diving under the water to find him, we could not. We had both surfaced and were trying to think of what to do next when Phillip accidentally trod on Dallas's head—luckily he had a long mane of hair and we were able to pull him up and swim him across to the other side of the river. We reached the bank and the ambulance arrived a few minutes later and he was taken to the local doctor's surgery.

Dallas never had any recollection of his fits and would just resume life where he was last placed. In this instance, when he came around at the doctor's office he said, "What are we doing here? Where are the girls?" Because someone with epilepsy breathes in very little during a seizure and the chest cavity actually squeezes air out, the lungs do not fill with water that would normally result in drowning. So while Dallas was under the water and because on both occasions he was taken out before completing the fit, his lungs did not take in any water that in other circumstances would have resulted in him drowning. The danger lies in the coming out of the seizure—being disoriented and without help in a dangerous situation such as a surf break could result in drowning, and that is what happened in Byron Bay. Just as life really seemed to be coming together for him he would again find the water during a fit; this time at a place for which I had such love and had experienced so many *wonderful moments in the same surf. Now, I would also experience one of my saddest as one of my best mates left the fold.*

There is no rhyme or reason to death. You just need to acknowledge those that you lose and rest in the knowledge that they may again evolve. You must also evolve in the here and now; remember, but don't spend your time in mourning—spend it living.

It is a belief held by some monks of the Buddhist persuasion which has been proven over time that they can choose the time and manner of their death. I believe this to be true and therefore hold no real fear of death as I know for me when that time will come and how it will take place.

Back to the City and More Football

A nother phone call from another friend would see me move back to the city, this time to the north of Australia and the city of Brisbane. Despite the laidback style of Byron Bay, I'd had a reasonably good year on the football field and represented the Far North Coast Division against a New Zealand Māori touring team. This had come to the attention of my brother from another mother, Changa Jones, and a much bigger club he was playing for at Redcliffe in Brisbane, the capital city of the state of Queensland.

I remained in Redcliffe for the next two years. It was good to catch up with Changa again and while I was there I forged lifelong friendships with fellow players and local community members. Brisbane is Australia's third largest city but back then it was more like a big country town when compared to our two major cities of Sydney and Melbourne. It suited me to some degree but when I had time and if I was not in the right frame of mind to play football and wanted a small break in my life I would invariably head back to Byron for a few days, surf a little and meet up with mates. It was during these two years I would endure the highs and lows of life as a footballer and also as a human being; a time to realise my own frailties, but not yet the time to act on them.

Weakness was something that had no place in my life—I had been conditioned throughout my life to be tough and resilient, to show that you were a man and not a wimp. I respect and am proud of my family and our name, but I was not the type of person that most people expected me to be. I would play out that charade for many more years to come and I think in hindsight I just didn't have the strength to be me. Exactly who that was or what form that person would take was also not clear to me. I just knew within that I was different from the perceptions others had of me.

It was also around this time that I recognised I was having occasional bouts of depression, or melancholy. I didn't really understand it at the time and masked it with alcohol. That is the worst thing you can do but still so many do exactly that and too many leave us far too early as a result. I was never treated or counselled for the condition and still live with the blue today from time to time as written earlier. I am a melanchologist, or as I would say, I live in the blue. Today and for the past 30 years I have been comfortable with that because I understand it and even at times embrace it—maybe because it shows that I am human and I do care. If you have no understanding of it (and I have met many throughout my life who fit that description), it can be a very dangerous animal.

As I said, Redcliffe held many highs and lows for me and although I was unable to recognise it at the time it also held many valuable life lessons that I would be able to look back upon, all helping to make me a better person. At the time I was still the party guy and for me life could not be taken too seriously but I did have feelings for others less fortunate and would always reach out to those in need. Although my life was far from ideal and partying was still the priority, I was starting to understand a very important word that I would carry forward: compassion. Some might call it feeling sorry for others—if so, they lack true understanding. Compassion is having a genuine concern for the wellbeing of others and, if possible, acting upon it, not just experiencing a momentary emotion.

From Redcliffe I moved back to Gunnedah for another year where I signed the first of three contracts to either play football for or coach my hometown team. I would also meet the young woman who was later to become my wife. But first, a little on football and its impact on my life.

Football

It's time to look at the role that football played in my life and the opportunities it afforded me; after this I will concentrate on life away from the field but because football shaped me in such a way and occupied so many years of my life, it most probably deserves some mention.

Throughout my time at Redcliffe I would represent at my highest level and also play at my lowest. During my first year at Redcliffe I hit the ground running and was highly motivated to do well as I was playing in the second tier of rugby league in Australia. The competition sat only behind that in Sydney, which every footballer aspired to. During the first year and after only a handful of club games I represented South East Queensland and from there the state of Queensland against the might of New South Wales. I would play against my cousin Dallas who was forging an illustrious career with Western Suburbs in the Sydney competition that would ultimately see him represent Australia.

There were three games played between the two states each year and they were largely dominated by New South Wales—in those days most of the best players from Queensland played in the Sydney competition and as such represented New South Wales. I played the first game of the series and injured my ankle; although I did play out the full game I was unable to train and was dropped for the second game. It is not clear if I would have been selected or not, injury or otherwise; I played a reasonable game but nothing outstanding.

**Premiership with Gunnedah and Captain of NSW Country
against Sydney City**

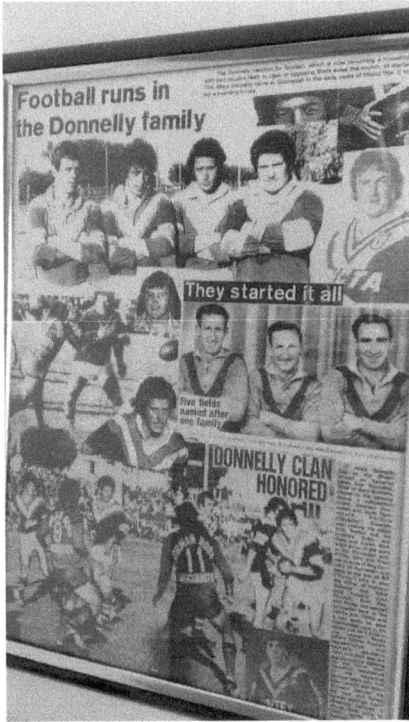

RUGBY LEAGUE ROUNDUP... RUGBY LEAGUE ROUNDUP... R

Queensland's lock Terry Donnelly

West's John Donnelly

Family at war!

By PAUL FENN

Donnellys to throw down the gauntlet

Terry Donnelly flew into Sydney with the Queensland Rugby League team yesterday, but he won't be meeting up with any relatives while in town.

The only family connection Donnelly has in Sydney is his cousin John — and the two will be opposed when NSW meet Queensland at the SCG on Saturday.

Terry Donnelly is the Queensland lock . . . John Donnelly, the bruiser from Western Suburbs, is a NSW prop.

"STAR OF '76"

Yesterday when the Queenslanders "went out on the town," Terry told coach Barry Muir he was not going anywhere near his cousin.

"He won't be paying any social call on the other bloke this week," coach Muir said.

"They won't meet until they get out on the Cricket Ground on Saturday, and you couldn't call that social."

Like his more famous footballing cousin, Terry Donnelly comes from Gunnedah.

He decided earlier this year to try his luck in big football and transferred to Brisbane, where he teamed up with the Redcliffe club — and coach Muir.

Since then he's battled his way into first grade and then the

Queensland State team with some outstanding lock-forward displays.

"Rugby League produces a couple of new stars each year, and I reckon Terry Donnelly will be one of them in 1976," Muir said yesterday.

Terry couldn't pick a worse time to come to grips with cousin John.

The big prop is playing outstanding football.

On Saturday he set about the Country forwards with a meanness which had his old team mates back-pedalling.

Then on Sunday he ripped into Balmain, despite some heavy strapping to a badly corked thigh suffered the previous day.

That injury, plus worries about second-rower Terry Randall and hooker George Piggins, will be checked when the NSW team trained at the SCG today.

I represented five separate New South Wales country divisions, winning two country championships and captaining the New South Wales country team against our city counterparts. I captained/ coached for three different country towns: Oberon, Leeton and Gunnedah (where I won a premiership as the captain/coach of my hometown team). I then played in another two premiership-winning teams under the tutelage of my good friend John Lennan before coaching Gunnedah to another grand final appearance.

One of the proudest moments of my career came in 1978 when I was fortunate enough to represent my hometown with three of my brothers, Brian, Garry and Philip, playing on the same team. Later I had the opportunity to also play alongside my youngest brother, Greg. Sports were once a very big thing in country towns and during my father's time there would be trains bursting at the seams as townsfolk from country centres travelled to surrounding towns to support their teams as they played. Gunnedah played for the Spicer Cup which, in our part of the country, was first played for early in the early 1900s. Times have changed and the prestige of playing for your hometown team may not be as it was; younger people now find different ways to entertain themselves and sport takes a backseat along with the pride of representing your town, something that was once held in such high esteem.

Football played a major role in my life, as it allowed me to establish friendships far and wide, and to live in towns and cities where I would not otherwise have lived. In those towns, for a time I had the opportunity to become part of those communities. I could play football but I don't think I ever gave football what it gave me. I just wasn't of the nature to be a warrior or to have the want and need for the success that others had and others longed for, and I think I played accordingly. I trained as hard or harder than most and when I played I gave my all for the team—although that was my all, it was not my everything. There is a slight difference, I could be up for a game but from day one my heart was never truly in it and I think that would be noticeable to an acute observer. I was picked to play for representative teams because I had some talent not because I wanted to be picked. I played because it took me places and to a degree it was expected that I would play, having the background that I did. I didn't play for the love of the game or because I wanted to excel—I was simply handed a family baton and ran with it.

After representing Queensland I was invited to meet with and then sign on and play for the South Sydney football club—a truly famous club that had produced so many champions of the game and still does to this day in the national competition. I enjoyed my time there meeting with some legends of the game and I admired the professionalism of the club and its players but it was not what I wanted or needed. The fact that one of Gunnedah's most famous footballers, John O'Neill, had also passed through these doors made it all very enticing. Would I have made the grade if I had pursued the opportunity? We will never know, and it's not something I dwell on; it just wasn't a fit for me.

Life is composed of moments that require your all, moments that require your full passion and commitment. Football, for me, was just a game to be played and enjoyed, a vehicle that took me to many unknown places and to make many new friends; a vehicle that also taught me what teamwork and friendships are really about. Gunnedah didn't win a premiership in 1983 because I was the captain/coach, we won because we had a lot of individuals whose skill and commitment was used to form a team and that team then unselfishly worked for each other. We removed the 'I' and focused on the 'we'. So it was that I never went to the big league—I didn't fail, I just didn't need it. I was content.

Teams are composed—as are families and communities—of many individuals who, when given a common purpose, can achieve most things in life if they play to their strengths. We all have roles to play and we need to acknowledge that; while as individuals we may all have different mindsets and skills, if we bring them together and meld them we can be formidable and make this world and our own little worlds much better places.

I would use this philosophy throughout life, later coaching junior and senior soccer sides and also, and most importantly, in Vietnam. Here, I needed to build a team of people capable of working together with one common goal: to enhance the wellbeing of these severely disabled kids who we have dedicated this portion of our lives to serve. To ensure that, this team needs those special ingredients required to get the job done: love, compassion, patience and understanding. That is our primary skill set and along with the professionals we bring in to help—my job is to coach, provide guidance and when outnumbered or in need of another strategy, find solutions. None of this is possible without staff input and they are all encouraged to take ownership of their individual programs, for if they own it, they will nurture it.

Football and life have a lot in common. My football background has served me well throughout life and the friendships that have grown, both through football and with my other teams, will last forever.

41

Gunnedah Again, 1978

This was a really enjoyable year for me and again cemented friendships that would last forever. I didn't dare live with my parents again as those days had well and truly passed, so I decided to share a flat with a new friend, Chris 'Paddy' Mellon. He was a real character and we formed a great bond in the year we spent living together. We would go each Monday to my mum and dad's house for dinner, something we really looked forward to as neither of us could really create any magic in the kitchen.

Mum used to look forward to us coming down and Paddy was always on his best behaviour there, spreading stories about some of things that I may have got up to and at the same time making himself out to be some kind of saint. He used to get a perverse joy out of telling me that my mum loved him more than me. I think the closest he came to being a saint was one time when he got drunk and wandered off to find somewhere to sleep, as he had a tendency to do, always leaving me and friends to try to find him and take him home. This particular night we had just about exhausted all avenues when we decided we should check the local Catholic Church and there, sure enough, sprawled out on one of the pews was Saint Paddy, fast asleep.

One day I was reading the local paper and it occasionally had a Page 3 girl; this particular day it was a young woman called Vicki Morrison. I didn't know her at the time but immediately knew that I should. She was in a bikini at the river for the shot and just looked absolutely beautiful. I knew even then that this relationship would be much more serious than any other. The opportunity to meet her arose at a local club dance night and I couldn't let it pass.

I introduced myself and asked her to dance but she told me that she could not as she had a boyfriend. I told her that I wasn't really concerned about that, but unfortunately she was, so it was not meant to be on that night—but it was meant to be.

The young man who was her boyfriend at the time, Mark, was a really nice guy and later a friend. Nothing happened between me and Vicki for the rest of that year, although we both knew that something may happen a little further down the road. We would bump into each other occasionally and chat, as happens in small towns, but that was the extent of our relationship. It's quite ironic that later I would marry Vicki, and Mark would marry the then sweetheart of Greg, my younger brother. I guess occasionally some things are just meant to be and have a karmic connection.

Newcastle and Oberon

I really enjoyed the year back home. We didn't win the competition, losing in the grand final, but we had an enjoyable year on the field and some great times off it. Life with Paddy was one adventure after another and it was nice to spend time with Mum and Dad, at a suitable distance. At the end of the season, I was offered a contract to play for a football team in Newcastle, so once again I packed my bags and moved on to a new city and team. I played for the Macquarie Scorpions in the Newcastle League and spent the year in the company of a wonderful lady called Vera who was a sponsor of the club. Vera sponsored my accommodation at her hotel and also gave me a job there. The only downside to it was that with Vera owning the hotel where I worked and lived I didn't search for the parties, they came to me. Vera was a wonderful, kind-hearted and generous lady who treated me just like a son; I will never forget her and the love she showed me.

Newcastle was new to me. We had a great supporter base, including the Nomad motorcycle gang; although I could never endorse their lifestyle or some of things I am sure they got up to, they were great supporters of the club and during my time with them I never saw them do anything untoward, although I am sure things did happen in their world that I really didn't need to know. I had a special bond with one of them, a man called Sharpey, and on occasions when we sat and talked alone he was much the same as anyone else that I knew. We all have frailties and weaknesses and it was amazing that he shared a lot of his personal life and feelings with me. It was amusing to slide over the try line and come face-to-face with a group of bikies cheering their heads off for you; I guess on game day it was good to have them on our side of the fence rather than the other.

Vicki and Mark had now finished their relationship and I received a message from her saying that she was coming to Newcastle and we should catch up. We did and would spend the next 27 years together. The season had finished and I had been offered the job as captain/coach of the Oberon football team in the western area of New South Wales.

I went to Oberon in late September just as we were entering spring and was surprised that it snowed when I was there but that was just a precursor to what in the next year would be a very cold winter. Oberon sits approximately 2,500 feet above sea level and at times it was so cold there that on some game days we played in the snow and actually wore plastic garbage bags under our jerseys to try and keep the warmth in. Oberon is a wonderful little town with a cold climate but also some of the warmest people on the planet living there.

Vicki had decided to come and join me there so we set up house on a farm about five kilometres out of town where the only companionship to be had were the cattle that also lived there and that we would occasionally pass as we all went about our daily routines. I kind of liked their company—they were not quite as complex as some humans I'd encountered and didn't really seem to care too much about anything. They led a simple life, but unfortunately one that rarely had a happy ending.

Life for us was also simple as there was usually just the two of us unless we invited friends out to eat and drink. The cold has a way of drawing people closer together, like the times you are with the one you love snuggling up under blankets with an open fire burning. The people and friends in town were really fantastic and we shared many evenings together either in their houses or ours, just relaxing and enjoying each other's company with everybody contributing to food and drinks. If you could adapt to the cold, everything about Oberon was good. But one winter would be enough for us.

During that year Vicki fell pregnant which put us in a quandary as to what to do. At that time it was always thought that one day we would marry but now we had to quickly make a choice as to when. Vicki at first wanted to marry immediately, before she showed a great deal, as she didn't fancy the idea of walking down the aisle with a slight bump; she later changed her mind and decided to have the wedding after the baby was born. As is the wont of women there would again be another change as Vicki experienced a feeling of guilt that the baby would be born out of wedlock. So, five months pregnant and fully showing we married in a small church in Oberon with only some family members and a couple of our local friends present.

The reception was a small dinner with close friends—about thirty in total—in the restaurant at the Leagues Club. Nobody was sure who had ordered a wedding cake so we walked in to find two of them on the main table. After we had eaten and gone through the small formalities of a wedding reception, we all went out to the main bar and enjoyed some drinks with the locals who were present and then went to the local RSL club where there was a dance every Saturday night. We had a wonderful time—everybody who was in the club, including some staff, formed a wedding circle and we went around the circle and got well wishes from what appeared to be almost everybody who lived in Oberon. Then we started the wedding dance and partied well into the night with a fantastic group of people.

I think small towns are very much like families, the community is the family and like all families there are disagreements from time to time but when there is something to celebrate, or somebody in a time of need, you wouldn't want to be anywhere else.

Leeton and a Special Gift

Leeton was the next town on my footballing odyssey—it was another small country town in the Riverina district, famous as a rice and fruit growing area. I think if you come to a place as a member of one of the town's major sporting bodies it gives you more access to the community as a whole and the different players that make up a town. That would again be the case in Leeton, with many lifelong friends to be had and assimilation into another family. We rented a nice little home on the edge of town as I prepared for a football season and Vicki was preparing for the birth of our first child.

That day came about quite quickly and it was then that I would learn about the true strength of women, both emotionally and physically. I guess, if truth be told, Vicki did go a little crazy during that mammoth eight-hour labour; she used a few swear words and I think at one point threatened to kill me if she was not given some drugs to stop the pain. I also felt I needed some drugs, as during the actual birth she squeezed my hand so hard I thought she would eventually break every bone in it. Time passed and soon the pain and anguish was replaced by joy, love and elation as we saw and held for the first time our son, Sam Donnelly. Sam was the first of our four children. To witness a newborn is an emotion that is very hard to describe, a small child that you, in part, created. I felt a sense of pride and love, just as I hold today for the man, son and brother he has come to be.

I was quite willing to stay another year or so in Leeton but with Sam now on the scene Vicki was determined to move back closer to family and so, once again, I returned home, this time for an eleven-year stay. While there, I would witness the birth, in quick succession, of two more sons, Jason and Matthew and, after a little break in time, our beautiful baby girl, Maddison.

Gunnedah—The Lows and the Highs

If life had intended that I have a period of time when I would experience the highs and lows it had to offer, then this was the time. Brisbane would seem like a kindergarten, now life was going to send me to college. This was also the time when life would offer utter clarity and show me a way forward that I had not previously thought possible; it didn't offer me riches of a material kind but rather riches of a personal and spiritual kind.

The obvious highs were the birth of a further three children and as with Sam I am just as proud of them today as I was the day they entered my life. Most kids will go through many trials and tribulations in their lives before they finally arrive at the right destination and my kids were no different; actually not that different in some respects to my younger life. The boys are now tradespeople operating their own successful businesses and my baby girl is no longer that baby, except in my mind and heart. She now works with her partner Leslie in her podiatry business and is leading a fulfilled life. So yes, I am very proud of them all and rest easy in the knowledge that they now accept my limited role in their lives and I also hope they share a little pride in me as their father. I could ask for no more.

Other highs included winning three premierships in a row with the local league side, once as the captain/coach and twice as a player. I knew this footballing life would have to end soon and at the end of each year I would announce retirement, then I would just as quickly begin playing again as soon as the next season started. I was once told that you are a long time retired so play as long as you enjoy it. I don't think I was particularly enjoying it anymore as the training that I used to love started becoming a chore and the bruises and aches from game day seemed to stay a little longer each year.

My solution was to go and play a different game, one that clashed on the same day as the league so that I could not possibly play league again. A very good friend of mine, Brian Lenton, was coaching the local Australian Rules football side, so it was there that I headed. I had an enjoyable year with a great group of people and won another premiership. I had played football since I was five years old but had to wait twenty-four years to taste my first premiership win and then, amazingly, it would be four in a row.

North West Aussie Rules Champions (standing, centre)

The lows were always around as it was a period of time when my melancholy went from blue to black for approximately six months. I was taking Valium to curb the depression and to halt anxiety attacks; I found it a little scary as I was unsure how to deal with it and at the same time present a different view to the rest of the world. What most do when suffering depression is try to mask it from the rest of the world until they really feel they can take no more and then a decision is made to either seek counselling and to tell the world; or for others, it is unfortunately sometimes to find peace in death. I was also agoraphobic during these dark periods, which meant I had a fear of open spaces, and that was hard to deal with considering I was a country boy and my job at the time required me to travel alone out to farmhouses in isolated areas delivering steel.

I think I only fooled myself if I thought nobody else in town knew how I was feeling, as I am sure almost everybody that was close to me did know. I had great admiration for Vicki during this period of time as I was really a lost cause, floating from job to job, and not really providing for the family as I should. Depression is a dangerous animal if let loose and for me it was running rampant. Vicki held us together and was, and still is, a great mother to our children. I'm unsure how I would have coped without her.

For people who find themselves living with someone in this state it is even more difficult as they cannot understand why you are as you are, and you yourself have little understanding. The only thing you do truly understand is that you want the sadness to go away but finding that way is often very difficult. You struggle with that until the day you finally acknowledge the why and then you can begin to deal with the issues that brought the black clouds in the first place.

The answers for depressive states are always there, it is just that some do not want to face and acknowledge the demons that brought this about. Because you are so angry with yourself and the person you have become, that anger can easily turn onto others, as it did in my situation. It was not a happy household to live in, especially for four young children.

The reality of the stage I went through cannot simply be whitewashed over, for it affects so many people. Oddly though, like everything else in life, it had a surprising upside, as over the years it has allowed me to help many others going through a similar situation. In order for me to escape the blackness I had to really search for the truth within and then provide the solution to this self-imposed disease. I loved my wife and children so if I wanted to keep them and for them to live a happy life, one thing needed to change, and that was me.

The first thing I needed to do was to stop drinking alcohol and then take prescription drugs out of my life. You can never solve anything with a clouded mind and these two things did not allow for much clarity. In certain situations, such as that really black period I encountered, prescription drugs can have a part to play but when they become your crutch and you think you cannot walk without them they actually make the depression deeper because now you feel the guilt of taking drugs to function in the world.

A small word of advice for aspiring mums and dads: don't be the 'don't do what I did' parent, be the 'do as I did' parent; the first doesn't really work, you have no fall back and if you would like to see your children moulded in a certain way, then be the good example, not the bad example. Think about the things you did and did not like in your childhood then take out the 'did not like' and give your children the parts that you did like. Eventually they will all find their own way, but occasionally they need someone to follow and advice rings hollow if you never heeded it yourself.

So one day it stopped. I decided I would drink no more and from that day forward I have not, with the only lapses being here in Vietnam. When I visit the house of an older person who is the head of the family they will usually offer a rice wine and to turn the host down would mean to turn my nose up at the family. So after explaining that I do not normally drink but out of respect for him and his family I will happily share one small wine, it is usually understood and well accepted and at times I never actually partake at all, we share a tea instead.

Stopping was easy for me as I was never a big drinker—I never had alcohol in the house and rarely drank during the week. I just liked to party on weekends and I guess those occasions more than made up for the missed weekdays. Later I joined the Alcoholics Anonymous family and also went there in another role. When I attended the meetings and heard the many stories to be told— some funny, some terribly sad, stories of alcohol destroying families and livelihoods, occasioning death and for some it even meant time spent in jail—I soon realised that I was an alcoholic. Like so many others in our society it is not necessarily the need for the drug on a daily basis but it is your inability to stop once you start. My downfall was on weekends and I did not want to stop once I started—one or two beers had no favour with me.

There is never any going back in life but if I could change one thing it would be to never to drink alcohol in the first place—it is a demon that is responsible for taking more lives than any other drug in the world. It destroys families and sometimes even communities. It was easy to stop but much harder to withstand the peer pressure that comes with that, especially in a beer-drinking nation like Australia and a small town like Gunnedah. I used to gain inspiration to stay dry simply from watching my mates with whom I would normally be drinking get completely drunk as I once did, then carry on like fools, as I certainly had. It was like holding up a giant mirror and made my desire to stop drinking even stronger and much easier.

It must be pretty difficult to counsel people when you have not had the experiences that they are going through; a book and teachings can only give you so much information and strategy. I wouldn't recommend drinking, using drugs or entering into a depressive state as a way to become a counsellor but I did find it beneficial to have fought the demons already when counselling others. I could more realistically relate to what they were going through, as I had actually experienced the pain and now the clarity.

Father Shenahan was the local Catholic priest and a wonderful down-to-earth man who had a relationship with my younger brother Garry, not through the church but surprisingly through gambling and drinking. Father Shenahan liked to partake of just a small amount of beer and had what we would call 'a little tinkle on the ponies' (horse racing) most Saturday afternoons at a local hotel. Here, he would meet up with my brother, who had similar wants and it was through Garry that I would meet and do a little work with the Father. He confided in me that he had occasion to counsel some young people from around town regarding recreational drugs and alcohol abuse and told me that he couldn't really relate to them as he would like because of the age difference and also his lack of knowledge of drugs. I agreed to help out and meet with these young people, listen and chat with them and, together with the Father, would take them to Alcoholics Anonymous in the hope that some of the stories would shake them up a little, and that the forum would also give them an opportunity to talk and open up about their young lives.

It is amazing the number of people who find themselves in alcohol and drug situations not because they like either but to mask greater problems in their lives that need to be rectified. If your hair is a little long and you want to change it and tidy it up a bit, you get a haircut, remove the unwanted hair and groom it into a style that suits you. It is not that easy to rid yourself of negative emotions or bad habits but if you cut away the root causes a little at a time and have patience, you will arrive at the style of life you are happy with.

One morning at around 2 am I received a phone call from a friend to ask if I would go to a certain house as his uncle was threatening to kill himself and had already self-harmed. The police had been called but he said he would not let anyone in the house except me and his nephew. I arrived to find the uncle sitting on the lounge room floor with blood seeping out from a wound he had already made by stabbing a knife into his upper thigh. He had removed the knife and was threatening to stab it into his other leg. There was little I could do as he held the knife and threatened that if anyone came near him he would also cut them up, so all I could do was listen to how he had ended up in this situation, reason with him a little and wait until either the alcohol he had consumed put him to sleep or the loss of blood had the same effect.

The ambulance people were waiting outside the house with the police for a call to enter. It was almost two hours that we sat and talked before the tiredness overcame him and he told me he wanted medical help. He was placed in the ambulance and taken off to hospital and I returned home. I don't think telling his true story about how he arrived at this point would be of any value right now—he was just somebody who was really down on his luck and, like that period of time I had gone through, depression and alcohol were playing their part. We are very fragile as human beings no matter how strong we appear to be and over the years ahead I spent many hours listening to others and offering the best advice I could, based upon my experience and understanding.

To feel the pain of others, is to understand compassion
To give pain to others, shows no understanding at all
Zet

Not long after I set drinking aside I came across a book called Zen Flesh – Zen Bones, *a collection of Zen and pre Zen writings compiled by Paul Reps and Nyogen Sensaki, a book I still have today some thirty odd years later. It is basically a collection of Zen koans [riddles] by various Zen (a form of Buddhist practice) masters. They are riddles that have no definitive meaning and no definitive answers—no right, no wrong, just what you feel and your interpretation.*

Occasionally, even today, if I am feeling a little lost I will randomly pick a page in the book and read the first koan I see and it always appears to relate to my particular situation. The answer is always in the koan; as it comes down to your understanding, the answer that you seek can always be found. In life, we may all perceive things in a different manner and we may also all have different opinions but there is rarely a right or a wrong. The answer to everything can be found in our own individual understanding of a particular event or person and also relies on our willingness to retain an open mind and to accept that sometimes we do not know it all. There are many things that take a deeper understanding but if you are not prepared to dig that little bit deeper, you may be as shallow as your perception.

From that book came many others related to Buddhism and its practices and meditations. Unfortunately, you do not turn into a Buddha overnight; that can take many lifetimes. And, also unfortunately, you do not find peace of mind overnight; that can take many years. But it was a start and a far more positive way of living my life than anything I had tried in the past. Buddhism and its guiding principles and meditations became a very important element of my life moving forward and I would wholeheartedly embrace it, and also go on a little magical mystery tour of my own.

The keys to peace are not always written in books for you, nor do they exist before you discover them; everybody should have their own way. You need guidance to begin with but then you must write your own book, discover what works for you in this life (and, importantly, is not harmful to others). The most important person in the world is you; if you function in a good manner then all around you benefit. If you are broken, you just add more to their sorrow.

We all must be students for a time
Then we become teachers of experience gained
If all you know is what you read or hear from others
Then your progress has not been as it should
Write your own book, after all, you are you

Zet

My mother had some news to share with the family, a secret that was hidden from her for more than fifty years and something that would impact each of us in the family in varying degrees depending upon how fully we embraced what was about to unfold before us. This explanation may take a little time so I hope you can bear with me.

You may recall me talking of the wonderful times spent with my grandmother; although those times would never change, our relationship status would. My mother grew up with two brothers, Sol and Archie and although they didn't live in Gunnedah during my youth, I remember their visits maybe once yearly, as well as the times we went to visit Uncle Archie at his home in the little hamlet of Anna Bay on the New South Wales coast. They were really good times—the ocean, swimming, a different means of fishing, collecting seafood and a completely relaxed lifestyle. The part I enjoyed the most may seem a little trivial but it was the outdoor shower that we would use to wash away the sand and salt after a swim in the ocean. I also enjoyed catching up with my cousins, Margaret and Helen. When Mum's truth was revealed, I would learn that they were actually my aunties.

Archie was a bricklayer by trade and he used to especially enjoy going up to the Aboriginal reservations in Arnhem Land in the Northern Territory to work. He did seem to spend a lot of time up there, especially later in his life. I always remember during his visits to our house how he would perform Aboriginal traditional dances and play the didgeridoo.

Uncle Sol was a travelling carnival/circus worker and as kids it was always a real treat when he came to town as we knew we would have some free tickets to whatever show he was with at the time. If he happened to work on a Pluto Pup or fairy floss stand at the carnival then that was also a bonus. Of course we loved to see him because we loved him, but he was a real enigma to us and would always arrive in town in the little van that he called home and would seemingly leave just as quickly once his show had finished. He travelled from to town to town all around Australia for most of his lifetime.

Unfortunately, time passed for these two wonderful gentlemen and the first of them to leave us was Uncle Archie. I still like to remember his wondrous joyous nature, his laughter and performance of those Aboriginal dances for us. Uncle Sol continued his visits and during one would reveal a truth to my mother that would cause shock and confusion in her life for some time to come. As the last member of Grandma's family Sol was duty-bound to tell my mother a truth, something I think was arranged a long time ago between Grandma, Sol and Archie.

Uncle Sol told my mother that there was another member of the family, a sister of his and Uncle Archie's called Thelma. When my mother relayed the story to us she said that as a very young girl she did remember Thelma in the household and that she was always bedridden and passed on due to a disease of which my mother, being very young, had no knowledge of. For Mum, Thelma was a blurred memory as she was so young at the time she could barely remember her at all. Sol would tell Mum that Thelma was not her sister but was, in fact, her mother and that both he and Archie were actually her uncles. The lady she had spent her life calling mother was in fact her grandmother. My mother's father was an Aboriginal man called Norman who lived in a nearby town called Tamworth but he had never had any contact with the family after his liaison with Thelma. This secret had been kept from my mother for over fifty years and she held the secret from us for five more years after Uncle Sol relayed the truth to her.

The reason my mother's past was hidden from her for so long was related to government policies in relation to Aboriginal people that were in place at the time. These policies were a form of genocide that saw Aboriginal people placed on reservations, some forced into slavery. There were also many massacres, with one of the most documented being the Myall Creek massacre that was committed not far from my hometown. Some Aboriginal people were poisoned and the children taken from their extended families. If you wanted to leave a reservation you had to sign a document forgoing your status as an Aboriginal person and could not have any further contact with other Aboriginal people, including your own family; all language needed to be forgotten, this was part of the process the government put in place for the whitening of Aboriginal people. Even if someone was willing to go through this process, they still had no right to vote until 1962.

There was not much difference between what happened in America, South Africa and here, but still many Australians prefer to pretend it never happened and our educational curriculum largely ignores the atrocities that occurred. You did not want to be an Aboriginal person in those days. If the truth could be hidden, it would be and so it was with my mother's story.

**There is no racial equality. There is that basic inequality.
These races are, in comparison with white races—I think
no-one wants convincing of this fact—unequal and inferior.
Edmund Barton, Australia's first prime minister**

My mother was born in the 1930s and her Aboriginality was kept from her for several reasons, the main being that if she was acknowledged as being of Aboriginal descent and with her light skin, under the Assimilation Policy she may have been forcibly removed from the family and not had the loving upbringing that she did. The idea of assimilation had been around since the 1930s but was not adopted as an official government policy towards the Aboriginal peoples until the 1950s, though there were no denials that 'unofficial' removals had been occurring since the beginning of the century.

Stolen Generations

Between 1910 and 1970, many Indigenous children were forcibly removed from their families as a result of these government policies. The generations of children removed under these policies became known as Australia's Stolen Generations. They were taken away from their families because the government did not believe in the future of the Aborigines; they thought their lives would be better under white institutions. Many methods were used to separate Aboriginal babies and children from their families.

The stolen children were raised on missions or by foster parents, totally cut off from their Aboriginality. They were severely punished when caught talking their Aboriginal language or talking to other Aboriginal people, they were to be completely isolated from their families and communities. So would begin the whitening process. They were taken to institutions where they were more or less imprisoned to be trained as domestics or labourers. The church also played a major role in carrying out this policy.

**To deny people their human rights is to challenge
their very humanity**
Nelson Mandela

**Darkness cannot drive out darkness; only light can do that.
Hate cannot drive out hate; only love can do that.**
Martin Luther King, Jr

It is not my intention to dwell any more on these policies nor on the completely racist society of the time but rather to show that there were many people caught up in the Stolen Generations. My mother was one of those children and so was I. Although my mother was not whisked off to an institution but instead was brought up in a happy household, she had her culture stolen from her. She had a father who she would never meet—who lived barely eighty kilometres away—stolen from her and she had five brothers and sisters stolen away by having to live a lie. They were her family and also mine. The Aboriginal culture that I now embrace was stolen from me for thirty-two years, and from my mother for well over fifty years. So on this day of revelation, the initial reaction of all of the family was much the same.

One of disbelief and confusion. Who I believed I was, is now changed forever.

*****

A year or so later, I discovered the identity of Mum's family in Tamworth and asked her if she wanted to meet with them. Obviously this was a very confusing time for her, as it was for me, but I cannot imagine what had gone on in my mother's mind when all of this happened. This was something that could really unhinge anybody but my mother seemed to have come to terms with her past and said that she has only one way to remember her family, and that was the way that she grew up; that she should not change that, as she was also afraid of the unknown.

Out of respect for Mum, I would not go and meet the family against her wishes; both the estranged family and I would need to wait until my mother was prepared to do so. They, of course, knew nothing of what my mother had been told but they did know of their sister in Gunnedah, and of her sons.

After another five or so years, Mum's curiosity got the better of her and she arranged to meet the family for lunch in Tamworth. Unfortunately, some three years earlier her father had passed away. She met with the family and had a wonderful day, a day, I am sure, when many other secrets were revealed; if so, Mum keeps them to herself. The sisters had a stall at Gunnedah's local markets on

Sundays, where they sold some products, so it was great that Mum still had the opportunity to meet and spend a little time with them.

Mum did tell me that her father Norman knew of his daughter and her sons and that he would occasionally make the trip to Gunnedah to watch us play football and he saw almost all of the games that we played in Tamworth. It must have been heartbreaking for him to sit in the stands or on the hill and watch his grandsons play but not be able to talk to them at all. I like to think he would have been a proud man watching those games and when I found out that he did see us play it made me feel good to know that in some way we did share something and although not verbally or physically, we did have contact. Maybe one day after a game he shook my hand and said, "Well played"; I don't know, but I like to think so.

I did speak to Aboriginal elders in town about all of this and they all said that they knew of the events and connections but for much the same reasons as my grandmother, everyone kept the secret, which is the Aboriginal way. Some things should not be spoken of and are best left to rest. That is a point of view I have of many things, both past and present: some things are better left unsaid.

Central Coast: Rearing a Family

Gunnedah was a fine town, a great place for me to experience my childhood, as it was for my kids in their early years. However, I really could not see a great number of opportunities in Gunnedah for my three sons and daughter later in life; it was a place where there would be limited work options for them. If they wanted to work in a particular field that was not available to them in Gunnedah they would need to leave the town or accept what was and, like me, they may later have a yearning to see what lay outside this small town. My oldest son Sam was about to move to sixth grade at school and a year later would be starting high school. High school can be a very daunting experience but if you graduate with a lot of friends it eases the fear a little. When you are twelve years old and some of the other students in the school are approaching eighteen it can have an emotional impact if you are tested by those older kids and harder if you go through that alone.

We decided to move to Central Coast, New South Wales, a lovely beachside area that lies between the two major cities in the state, Sydney and Newcastle. Sam would have one more year in primary school to gain some friendships and the opportunity to move to the bigger school with a group of friends that he was comfortable with, then our other kids would follow suit. The Central Coast was also a growth centre and with Sydney and Newcastle both short commutes, I knew that they would have work opportunities close by.

The early years were great, as the kids made new friends and sampled what the coastal lifestyle had to offer. For me, it was also a good place to live as I loved the surf and fishing, and both activities could be shared with the kids, so any downtime was usually occupied by those pursuits. That would not always be the case as the kids reached their teens and found their own friendship groups and wanted their independence. We would share less time together in my pursuits and they had other things on their agenda as they slowly matured. My little girl Maddy was five years younger than our youngest son Matt so she would eventually become more of my constant companion than the boys.

Time with the boys was usually spent through sport. I would see them in the surf occasionally and spend time with them and their friends but they were far more skilled than I. When I first surfed in Sydney all those years ago I started with a short board, but on the coast I moved to a long board, then a boogie board and eventually no board, just a pair of flippers and I think that was when I was happiest. There was something surreal about just swimming into a wave and following its flow as it broke onto the shoreline; it was as though you were actually a part of the wave and one with nature. Waves all vary, none are the same and that was also part of the challenge—to read the wave, to determine which way the break would benefit you the most and to remain in the unbroken face for as long as you could. Using only a pair of flippers and my body enhanced the surfing sensation for me.

I coached Sam in rugby league, Jason and Maddy in soccer, and Matt in both. I loved coaching soccer as it wasn't as brutal as rugby league and it was a game that, while the player obviously needed good technical skills, the coach also had to be a good tactician; for me it was a little like playing chess. I was sitting and watching Jason play one day and thinking to myself and also asking Vicki, why doesn't the coach do this or that, or change this position or that position—a typical parent I guess at your kids' sporting events. I never needed my kids to be superstars, I just wanted them to enjoy sport as part of their growth and to understand the meaning of teamwork and, to a certain degree, discipline. I also did not want to be one of those parents sitting on the sideline condemning a volunteer coach—if I thought I could do it better, then I should do it.

The following year I successfully applied to coach Matt's under-14 team at the Killarney Vale Soccer Club. We had a hugely successful year and became the first club from the coast to win the state champion of champions title; we were the best side in our state at our age level. It was an interesting year as we competed in the local competition and had to occasionally travel to other regions for Cup games. We quite easily won the Central Coast competition but didn't really know if the state title would be within our reach. We went off to the finals in Sydney just happy to be there. We were huge underdogs—the team from Sydney we were to play in the final had been undefeated for the past five years; but we won! I never debate how much influence the coach has on a team's success—certainly to some degree—but for me it was always about next year and what the kids carry forward. If the young person you are coaching still has the same skillset and the same understanding of how the game is played, what have you achieved?

I wanted each member of the team to develop as a player over the course of the year I was with them and to have a better understanding of the game than they had previously. If they needed coaching more in the technical aspects I would find someone who would teach them what I could not; after all, I had only ever played one game of soccer in my life. It was my job to see that they were happy—they were only kids out for a kick around and if they were happy together they played for each other, not for themselves. We were very happy that year and it's wonderful that I still meet with these young adults and can call them friends.

I remember one night I took them to the sheds for a chat, as I thought we needed a little inspiration. So I asked one of the players, Ryan O'Connor, to walk across the shed just as he normally would. Ryan happily did that, then I invited him to walk back across the room but to close his eyes before doing so and imagine that he was Superman, the Man of Steel, and then open his eyes and walk as he thought Superman might. Ryan did it, with a very notable change from a carefree, devil-may-care kid to a supremely confident and virtually indestructible young man;

he strutted across that room like nothing in the world could harm him and he was capable of doing anything. The next Saturday we had a team of supermen, and so it progressed until season's end. No matter how trivial it may seem, everybody needs some self-belief and how we get it doesn't really matter, as long as we believe in ourselves and are happy with the person we are.

Sadly, in 2019 during the writing of this book, we lost Ryan as he reached a point where the obstacles that life can throw at you all became too much for him. Like many others with personal, alcohol, drug or mental health issues who need peace and truly believe within themselves that they cannot find it here, it seems that there was no other way out. I loved Ryan as I love my own children and we talked on the phone only a couple of weeks before his death about the issues he was facing and had encountered. I was in Vietnam so we were far apart and could not spend too much time talking and at the time of his passing I wondered how different it may have been had I been closer. I also understand that is not something I should dwell on, we had our moments and it was just one crazy day/night that nobody could have predicted that led to Ryan's demise and at that time he had friends and family near him if he needed (wanted) to talk, it was just his time, his choosing. The last words he said to me were 'I love you, Tex' and mine to him, 'I love you too, Ry'; words I will carry when I think of that young boy walking across the room as Superman. I feel blessed that our last words were words so powerful and meaningful.

If you keep filling a balloon with air it will burst and the only way to prevent that is to release some of the air, a little at a time. A balloon can only take so much and it is the same with human beings. Like Superman and kryptonite we all have frailties; we need to acknowledge them, find help and release them.

A week after Ryan's death I also received news of the death of another young man and friend I had coached. I coached him as a youth and was saddened to hear of his demise, and that it too was related to alcohol abuse. He was a lovely young man, admired by all who knew him. There have been others, some I knew, some friends of my kids and family; it's so sad to see the youth of today finding it increasing difficult to live in this world.

The same month we also lost two kids from the disability centre in Vietnam while I was in the process of helping another young man deal with his depression and related issues here in Vietnam. It was a difficult and emotional month, but I am still living, so I am the lucky one. I just needed to release each in my own way.

After coaching Matt's team, the next year I went on the same journey with Jason, winning the local competition and just falling short at the semi-final stage of the champion of champions competition, but still a great effort to get there. I would coach Sam for a year in rugby league, although with limited success. I guess at that time I had seen and played enough of that game to not be motivated enough to motivate others.

I moved on to do some representative coaching in soccer and spend time with Maddy, who was also quite an accomplished player. I coached her in local representative sides and we travelled together as she represented the state at school level. If we weren't moving around with soccer, we were catching fish together under the Entrance Bridge. I had some wonderful years with that young lady, my baby, and also the boys as they started to mature into the adults they are today. I willingly share love with all I meet in my life, no matter their race, religion or beliefs, but no greater love do I have than that for my children.

That love is obviously tested over the years as they move into mid-teens and young adults; this can be a testing time for both children and parents as your kids discover a different way of life and you try to keep them away from the evils you know exist. My kids, like me, were not academically minded; they all wanted to leave school at around the age of sixteen—I guess they thought if they could work then they could also play. History was about to repeat itself but I had a different role.

I didn't argue with my kids about leaving school for I believed if I forced a young teenager to do the things they didn't want to do then they would rebel, learn nothing and I would have an unhappy child and a soured relationship to deal with. I had one stipulation regarding this, and that was that if they left school they could only leave if they engaged in an apprenticeship, as I wanted to ensure that as they grew into young adults they had security in their lives and an occupation that would not only reward them well financially but also give them an option for further growth.

My experience in regard to employment was most certainly not what I wanted for them—jumping from job to job with little opportunity of securing a good financial foundation. I don't regret for a second how I have lived my life, although I guess as I moved from town to town it would have been much better if I could have done that as a tradesman, not just as a footballer. These three lads were no longer my little kids, they were maturing and each was an individual and needed to be treated as such, with an amount of respect due. It was time for them to make choices and for me to simply offer advice that I thought would benefit them the most.

So I personally contacted people through my various friends in sport and the community, and secured each an apprenticeship with people I trusted. Sam would study carpentry, Jason tiling and Matt landscape gardening, Matt would later do some further study and join his brother Jason as a tiler.

I had many proud moments with my kids as they grew into young adults and of course many moments of angst as they strayed off what we as parents see as our preferred pathways for them, but I took special pride in the way they adapted to their apprenticeships. They lived in a coastal environment that was renowned not only for its surf but also for the culture that usually comes with the gathering of a lot of young coastal people—parties, alcohol, drugs, rock and roll. It was typical of a coastal environment and for young people something was always happening; if not, you found a way to make it happen. They partied but they rarely missed a workday because of their lifestyles and they all went through their apprenticeships without any major hurdles. Today, through their efforts and their commitment to those trades, they now have an opportunity for a financially secure life.

Maddy also left school early and moved to Newcastle to work in a carpet/furniture shop owned by her auntie and uncle. I was happy enough to see her do that as she would be with family and it made me feel secure knowing that. Life for her during her time there would also have its ups and downs, and she needed to mature much quicker than a young girl should have to. I always took pride in her compassion for others and also in her personal inner strength, for those years came with difficulties and have a story that only one person can tell and that is not me. She married and now lives and works with her partner Leslie and has found true happiness and security; with her personal happiness also comes my happiness.

I am sure if all were asked when the happiest time we had as a family was it would be in a rented house in Charlton Avenue, Toowoon Bay. It was an old timber home, quite large, but we now had late teenage and early twenty-year-olds who wanted their own space. So, as often happens, Maddy as the youngest ended up with her bedroom being in a semi-public area of the house; she was not too happy at first but adapted as time went by. The house was only 200 metres from Toowoon Bay, a beautiful little bay that rarely had any waves of note but was an ideal place to chill and forget what ever troubles you may have.

I used to go there in the mornings before work or evenings and meditate. I would lie on my back in the bay, close my eyes and just let the current move me as I went to nothingness. I would usually come out of this peaceful state if I happened to fall asleep and sink, or if a wave came that was a little bit bigger than most. Of course in both instances it usually resulted in me coughing out copious amounts of salt water but the moments of serene peace made it very worthwhile.

I had changed quite a lot. I was very much into nothing, my mind was usually at peace and very little bothered me. I stopped swearing when I was thirty-two years old as I found it was just a negative way to express myself and I was on a mission to remove all negativity from my emotional being. My other alone time, which I was also quite happy to share with others if they came along, was sitting out on the back porch at night, usually with a cup of tea or coffee and just staring at the beautiful sky that nature provided for me. I would see one or more shooting stars cross the sky on most nights. At the side of the porch was a frangipani tree that provided a beautiful scent to further enhance the atmosphere.

Nature, to me is very spiritual so it is very sad to see today what we are doing to our environment. We do have keepers who give of their time valiantly to make change but unfortunately not enough of them to effect major change. Governments govern us and big business governs governments, so unfortunately we are all at the mercy of corporations who have only one thing in mind.

In the house we had a few simple rules: one was to stop swearing, no drinking to excess and show respect to the family in general and to any visitors we may have. To implement a no swearing rule in a house full of these young adults was always going to be difficult and I didn't have any high expectations but to my surprise, it worked and soon we had a family who, after a slip of the tongue, would apologise for swearing; even now as adults with children of their own, they still do the same to me. It may sound a little strange to some but if the truth be known our house was a much happier place without it. I have only felt anger and sworn on four occasions since those times and they were all with my eldest Sam. Again, nothing to be written here but we both understand why and how those occasions happened and have worked, as always, to resolve them.

Happiness is sometimes also accompanied by sorrow and Sam went through a very difficult time in his life during our time in Charlton Avenue; the road back from there has been difficult for him. It is so hard to see one of your own suffer and really feel completely useless to help in the way that you would like to and also to have to make equally difficult decisions regarding that suffering so that it would not affect all family members.

Sam and his two best mates, Kenny and Troy went on their first overseas adventure together in October 2002; unfortunately, that time would coincide with what was to be known as the Bali bombings in Indonesia, a time when over 200 people lost their lives in two separate bomb explosions. It was the first time—and I think the only time when drinking alcohol—has done Sam any favours.

He was drinking with the boys at Paddy's Pub but had had his fill and decided to leave; as he walked back towards the hotel he was stopped by a local man whom he had met earlier who asked Sam if he would like a cigarette. Sam agreed and sat and chatted with him as they enjoyed their smokes near another bar called the Sari Club.

Within moments of sitting he heard a large explosion which was one of the suicide bombers detonating a bomb in his backpack at Paddy's Bar; this was quickly followed by a second explosion from a car bomb detonated just outside the Sari Club, in close proximity to Sam. We heard on the news what had happened and we knew that the boys would be out in one of the bars over there. The not knowing was very difficult—*is our son alive or dead?* Thoughts run rampant until you actually know, so when he called and we heard his voice on the phone we shed tears of relief and happiness.

We spoke with Sam on the phone as soon as he was able to contact us and although still obviously in a very confused state he was concerned about his mates and wanted to look for them. In Bali itself everybody was told to remain indoors and although we also had concerns for Troy and Kenny we didn't want Sam running to search for them when nobody actually knew if there would be more bombs or not. It was a difficult conversation for all and what could we really do or say when we were so far removed from the terror as it unfolded that night?

Kenny and Troy had also had quite a lot to drink and fortunately for them they had left the main crowded indoor area and were outside to the rear of the building when the bomb exploded. They tore themselves up a little climbing over the rear wall to escape. Luckily for all of our families, the boys came home to us; over 200 others did not.

Sam and I spoke briefly of the events that happened in Bali and although I wanted him to open up more about it he did not want to and he attended only one counselling session provided by the government to all victims. Although I tried to get him to talk to others because I knew how it would benefit him, he refused. We all have our own way of how we think we can deal with tragedies in our lives but I knew that closing up shop was not the way to do that. Still, if the person does not want to talk there can be no other option but for them than to deal with the demons in their own way; as it turned out it was, and still is, for him a nightmare not too distant. The next year and a bit would be extremely hard, as I am sure some nights now for him still are. As a parent, it was hard to sit by and watch it unfold. I am lucky that I have never witnessed such dire events in my life and if that never happens then I will be eternally grateful.

I would think it was similar to coming back from a war zone for Sam. My father fought in World War II against the Japanese in Papua New Guinea and throughout most of his life would wake in a cold sweat from nightmares about what he experienced there. I am sure that in moments alone he would also have thoughts that he wished would just disappear. Like most returned servicemen, it is not just the war that you fight but the battle you have internally when you return.

This also created a different life view between Sam and me, but one that was not spoken of that often. Sam came back with hatred in his heart and anger in his mind for all Muslims and released that hurt on others in a number of ways that he should not have. Again, to me, understandable given the situation, but still these types of behaviours had to stop, and would. Time, understanding and compassion from all close to him were needed. I had to make some hard decisions that I thought were in the best interests of all our family members. Those decisions were made and after a time of pain and anguish, Sam and I moved on and share a special bond and mutual respect; we are as a father and son should be.

Sam had an extreme hatred for Muslims and I had a different view, but we never clashed over that. In this book it is not my intention to speak specifically about the problems the world and Australians have with people of a Muslim background and the Islamic religion. But it has had a profound effect on me and my family in a very personal way, so I feel I should relate my views. My son was attacked by a small number of Islamic extremists; he was actually in the country that has the largest population of Muslims in the world, of which all but a small minority group condemned these attacks. Thousands upon thousands of Australians still fly to this Muslim country for their holidays each year and are welcomed, but although an increasing number of Australians are happy to holiday there, some do not want these people or their religion in our country. I would never place a blanket over any religion or race for the actions of a few and if I was to do that then I would have very few friends in my homeland as I would say the most extreme terrorists in my country and most other Western countries are white Christian people.

There have been three mass shootings involving or directly related to white Australians. The first occurred in Port Arthur, Tasmania in 1996 and saw the brutal murder of thirty-five people, with another twenty-three wounded, at the hands of Martin Bryant. The second attack in 2019 saw an Australian, Brenton Tarrant, go to New Zealand and cold-bloodedly murder fifty-one people as they prepared to pray. The latest, again in 2019, was in Darwin, where Ben Hoffman went on a killing spree, murdering four people, although the police stated this was not a terrorist attack. If he was Muslim, would it have been?

Every day around the world there are numerous murders, rapes, bashings and indecent acts against children by those we should trust the most. Some people are too scared to walk the streets for fear of assault.. I think I have, more than most, a reason to feel anger and hatred against Muslims; the actions of a few took away the happiness of my young son and replaced that with hatred and fear. But it was not a religion that did that, it was the actions of a minority, as those daily crimes committed at home are the actions of a minority group no matter what race or religion.

The only rightful occupants of my Australian lands are Aboriginal people. Everyone else here has a family tree that leads to another country and religion, and that includes me through my father's Irish heritage. The lineage of others either comes from the First Fleet or immigration. I really struggle to understand why people ignore that fact and can be so bitter towards people who just seek the same opportunities that everyone else was afforded. The more we provoke the more at risk we become.

I read a story last week from someone who said in jest that white people believe that they have one extra gene that is not present in ethnic groups; he called it a superiority gene. Yes, I had a giggle, but is there really any truth to that? I am sure there are some who believe it to be true.

**Racism is born from ignorance
And resides within the fool
May humanity be our race
May love be our religion
*Sa Chin ThAkur***

It is the way I live my life, and if you can too, then we are two and so it grows. If you feel you cannot, you are part of the problem. I don't expect the world to be one massive love-in but I would like to see people try to show a little more understanding and compassion towards their fellow human beings

Back to Charlton Avenue

I knew that I could not control what happened outside of the house; that was for the kids to learn and we often sat and spoke about that. They would be responsible for their decisions, mistakes would happen, stupid things would be done and eventually they would all decide the kind of life they would live. All Vicki and I could do as parents was to provide some guidance and be there as support when needed.

The Central Coast, while being a great place to raise children, also had its downsides. One of those was not being able to have a party to celebrate your children's coming of age at eighteen or twenty-one, as you would run the risk of a mass invasion and trouble aplenty. I had seen enough on social media of people's houses being taken over by wild teenagers the hosts didn't even know and sometimes their houses and fences being partially destroyed.

I knew that my kids were very popular throughout the community and that if one of the boys did have their twenty-first at home it would most certainly result in a huge number of unwanted guests arriving. So we all agreed on these occasions that a very few select friends and family would gather for dinner and a few drinks and then the birthday boy or girl and their friends would go on to party at one of the local clubs or hotels with as many people as they wanted.

One of those times when a large group of young people gathered to party the night away would soon come to us in a different and negative way. There were always reports in the local paper or on the news of beach parties getting out of control on the coast and police having trouble controlling the situation because of the sheer volume of young people who would turn up. We would have direct involvement in such a situation; a situation you hoped your kids would not be involved in but always knew it was a possibility.

At approximately 1 am one morning we received a phone call from the local police, telling me they had two of my sons in custody; I had to ask them to repeat what they had said as I was wondering if I was the subject of a prank. When it was clear that I was not, I just asked again, "Two of my sons?" They said, "Yes, Sam and Jason." I immediately went down to the station to see what had happened and find out why.

It turned out there had been a large beach party on our local surf beach, Shelley Beach, which got totally out of hand with around 200 youths attending; obviously the police had great difficulty and also short fuses as they tried to clear the area. One of Sam's friends had been thrown into the back of a paddy wagon and Sam had decided to act to help his mate; whether he was in a fit state to do so was at best debatable but if he had one strong character trait that was his loyalty to others. He ended up joining his mate in the wagon. Jason, upon seeing his older brother thrown in the wagon also decided to act, resulting in him unwillingly joining the others and all of them being driven to the local station. Matt, who was also there, had earlier found himself in the clutches of the police but, thanks to an intervention from Sam, was able to struggle free and take off into the bushes and quickly forgotten as the police struggled to disperse the rest of the crowd.

I later thought it was a shame that Matt had escaped, as we had a great opportunity for a family picture: my three sons behind bars. Of course, I say that light-heartedly but at the time it was anything but. I arrived at the station and the sergeant took me to the cell area where the boys were kept and sure enough there they were, with maybe another twenty youths, some of whom I recognised and others I did not. I spent a little time with some parents I knew who were in the same situation that I was.

The sergeant was trying to explain what had happened and as I knew nothing about the situation I was nodding my head and trying to appease him but this may have been a mistake. The boys obviously did not agree with his account of the night and were angry that I seemed to be agreeing with him so they and a couple of other kids started unloading their anger on him, and my boys on me, for supposedly agreeing with him. The sergeant suggested we move out to another area to discuss what needed to be done and I had no hesitation agreeing with him. He told me that he could release them to me now, or if not, they would release them at six in the morning; again with no hesitation, I said that I thought it best he release them in the morning.

They were still drunk and not in a fit state for any discussions; I wanted them to spend more time in the cell so they could take a little time to sober up and think about whether it was a place to which they would want to return. Sometimes it is best not to speak at all but leave someone who temporarily has the devil on their shoulder to have time to think long and hard about where their actions have led them. So, instead of taking two boys home who were in no mood to listen to anyone, I instead had two very humble and contrite boys arrive home four hours later; they were full of apologies and asking for guidance on what they should do to escape further penalties.

There was no point in being angry with them, for what had happened had happened and I couldn't change that; I just hoped that this night would provide some learning for how they would conduct themselves in the future.

Another time I had dreaded coming but I knew would, was the first time my little Maddy tasted alcohol. I was getting ready to sleep one night when I heard voices outside and recognised one of them as Maddy who had been out with friends to a birthday party. She was taking some time to come inside so I went out to see if everything was ok. There, laying on her back across the footpath, was my little baby—drunk as could be, talking loudly and laughing with that infectious laugh of hers. She was with a couple of her friends who were trying to get her up off the ground. I always knew that this moment would come; after all, she had three brothers who had led the way. I wasn't upset with her at all, just a little saddened that it had happened so early in her life at sixteen. But you cannot lock them in cages, they need some freedoms.

When events like this occur, it doesn't mean that you are a bad parent it simply means that you have teenagers who are experimenting and are at times influenced by their peers. They are going to make mistakes and don't need your anger; they need your support—this isn't about you, it's about them.

I spoke of Maddy's laugh because I love it so much; it is so genuine and every time I hear it I feel joy and happiness. The one thing my Maddy has that many people in life don't, is genuine friends and admiration from all who know her. She is one of those people you cannot help but like, or love—I know of no one who feels indifferently about her. Although we don't see each other too much nowadays, I still love those moments we talk on the phone and I hear that laughter. As much as I was saddened and she shocked when she saw me there, there was nothing to talk about; this day was coming and here it was. I helped her inside, laid her down to sleep and in the morning we had breakfast and a little giggle about what had happened, and of course talked of ways to prevent it from occurring again or at least with less consumption and certainly not on a regular basis.

These were isolated incidents that occurred; as I said, overall it was a very happy time in Charlton Avenue. We would usually have around nine people for dinner as the boys each had girlfriends who spent most of their time at our house and slept over most nights. Dinner was always special when the nine of us would sit down around the table and recount the day's events or things not long passed and other things soon to come. Maddy also gained some older sisters, which I am sure at her tender age was beneficial as she could now chat with her 'sisters' about female things and have a big sister's shoulder for those more personal moments.

Jason first met his girlfriend Emma when she was sixteen and married her some years later; they now have two beautiful sons, Eli and Nate. Although so young, her parents didn't mind her virtually living with us and we were happy to have her, our daughter number two. Maddy would find her partner Leslie a little later on, so we also have daughter number three. Sam has a lovely partner named Tash and two beautiful daughters Blakely and Ahlei, and Matt, while unfortunately splitting from his partner Ashley, has from that relationship a wonderful daughter in Daphne Heather and son in Peter. So we were a happy family and as parents we had to sometimes put up with their teenage testing behaviours and they also had to put up with a sometimes offbeat dad.

I was sort of in a zone, I guess a time zone of my own; there were certain things I had to do in my life on a daily basis to provide an income but I really enjoyed discovering the spiritual being that I am and we all are. I just wanted love in my heart and peace in my mind and I explored ways to make that happen, such as meditating in the water, spending nights with the stars and the frangipani tree; just going back to nature and discovering my own personal inner nature. You can only take so much from books you read and people you talk to, for there is a time when you need to be the true you.

I used to have silent days once a week, days when I just didn't talk. I'm not sure why I did this but I did enjoy them and I guess it also gave me an insight into how people who are mute communicate in the world as there are not many people in the general community who can use or understand sign language. I needed to be disciplined on these days. It also allowed me to see the reactions of others and the frustrations those close to me felt when I didn't speak, even though we would communicate in some form. If somebody close to me did the same I would have just said ok and not concerned myself about it but that is just my way—don't let the little things get to you.

So on these days I went about my life as normal, just not speaking and I found that I could get through life without any real hassle. Difficult, of course, if the phone rang on these days but I just didn't answer it; if I thought it may be important, I would send a text to find out. Occasionally some friends of the kids would see me at the beach or shopping centre and say hello and I would respond with a hand gesture to the throat signalling that I could not talk. They would inevitably later ask one of the kids if I was sick with a bad throat and my kids would usually just let them know that I was having a crazy day, doing my own weird stuff. Eventually all who knew me also knew about the days and usually just smiled and got on with their lives.

I was down at the beach one day and really fancied a whipped ice cream so I went to the man in his van; I showed him that I could not talk but pointed to the one I liked and was surprised when he gave it to me for free. I tried to give him the money but he wouldn't accept it and I couldn't explain to him what I was doing. He was just a kind-hearted man as were most that I encountered when trying to communicate in this way. I had no problems moving through the world with this slight impairment but am grateful I don't carry it permanently. There were some other crazy things I did in my pursuit of personal happiness but that's another story.

Over the years on the Central Coast I had many different jobs. I would do whatever was necessary to keep shelter over our heads and to put food in our mouths, and I was very lucky that most of those jobs were in areas where I was part of a team that helped others. Normally, I wouldn't last more than two years in a particular job as I would get bored or find that what I had been recruited to do was done and therefore somebody else could just as easily take the lead.

Approximately eighty per cent of your life is spent working and sleeping so make sure you are happy with your work life and try to live your life in such a way that allows you to sleep in a peaceful state free of guilt and regret.

I worked as a business consultant on a government program to help Aboriginal people start their own small businesses. I managed a team that started the first Aboriginal group training scheme in Australia, working towards finding apprenticeships and traineeships for Aboriginal kids in the mainstream sector. I was also part of a team that established the first Aboriginal foster care group in Australia and was the state manager for Aboriginal hostels. We provided accommodation for transient people and hostel accommodation for young students from remote areas to come to regional cities to advance their education. One of the most personally rewarding jobs for me was working with extremely disadvantaged kids for the Marist Youth Care agency.

Marist Youth Care was given the contract to care for approximately twenty-five teenagers who were deemed the most troubled and likely to re-offend teenagers in New South Wales. These kids were in and out of detention centres and similar programs to ours and were considered unmanageable. I was charged with the task of managing two homes for boys and overseeing another for young girls that would primarily be supervised by a female manager. These houses would contain only one young person or two depending upon their previous behaviours and would have at least one member of staff on site 24/7.

My first house was to contain one young person who I had seen only once during my induction in one of the houses in Sydney. He was very small in stature but always a keg of dynamite ready to explode, very devious and quite intelligent. He was moved to the coast from Sydney because the only thing he liked to do was to fish and it was the only thing that would keep him calm; if we could provide a happy environment it may aid in his rehabilitation. He had been housed on the coast for a week at a seaside park in a cabin but the management of the park kept getting complaints about his noise and swearing, so he had to leave. It was with a bit of luck, although with some reservations from the real estate agent, that we quickly found a house to rent at The Entrance, a suburb located near some good fishing spots that we hoped would keep a smile on his face.

I was yet to meet him on the coast as I was still undergoing induction in Sydney the week that he was moved. The following week I was returning to the coast from Sydney with every intention of going to the house to meet him and some new staff members when I received a phone call that would necessitate change. All I could hear on the phone were the sounds of sirens blaring—they turned out to be from fire trucks, as our little lad had burned down the rented house.

The most important thing a staff member is instructed to do is to never leave the kids alone in the house. It was the first night in the house and it was bare of groceries so with our young lad refusing to leave the house to go to the shops, the staff member, thinking that he would only be five minutes at most, took a risk—one that did not pay off. The house was a typical timber/fibro cabin that was common on the coast so all the lad had to do was build a small fire in one room and the old house would do the rest. He ran some way and then hailed a cab to take him to the local railway station where he hoped to jump on a train to Sydney. But when it became apparent that he would not be able to pay the fare the cabbie locked him in the car and had the police come and take him away. Unfortunately, it would be back to a juvenile justice centre for him, and for me, the hard task of going to the real estate office the next morning and telling them that in less than one day their new tenant had burned the house to the ground, despite the initial assurances from me that nothing like this would occur.

The other house accommodated two young people, both with a litany of offences behind them. These kids had been subjected to horrific abuses and only knew one way to exact any type of revenge, and that was through anger and any crime they could find to commit. To me it seemed that they knew the offences they committed would keep them away from their abusers and the greater the offence the more time they would be away. Both had been sexually and physically abused by family members or friends of the family, one by his uncle and grandmother.

I felt sick just thinking about the horrors they had in their short lives and although the offences they personally committed did affect others, I thought it was understandable why they would act out in that way. We should never judge on what we first perceive as there is always a story behind the why; but in general, we never really want to know. If you were the victim of one of their crimes it would be perfectly understandable why you would be angry and want justice because when anger arises we really don't care or want to know about the why.

When I was undergoing the induction process in Sydney I was taken to one of the houses containing two young people from similar circumstances to the two I was to look after on the coast. It was something of a shock to me when I approached the house as I was taken aback by the noise, primarily music blaring out on one of the kid's stereos—I guess you would call it punk or grunge music. You could also hear the staff trying to talk above the racket and a lot of swearing by all present. The kids were dressed primarily in black, which was obviously their choice, and their T-shirts had symbols of hate and violence on them. I really couldn't see or hear anything there of a positive nature that would in any way enhance the lives of these kids.

I decided the house I had responsibility for would in no way resemble this place and as soon as it was ready and occupied by our boys we had a meeting. The house was in a nice area and not too far from the coast. It was also of a reasonable size and had a good outdoor space—I would have been very happy to live there.

One of the boys was from the north coast and was sent to us because he couldn't be controlled and they hoped that a location further away from family would work for him. They were always concerned that he was going to run, so whenever he went outside or for a walk, a staff member followed; it was a little like being kept under constant surveillance, which in a sense, he needed to be but it also showed no trust. It was something he really detested and it produced anger and rage rather than diminishing it. So I told him that if he left the house while he was with us that we were not going to follow him; he would have twenty minutes to return and if he did not we would ring the police and he would be headed to a juvenile justice centre again. If he did anything wrong when out there we would again call the police and he would be sent to a juvenile justice centre.

It was not my intention to immediately call the police but I hoped it would be a deterrent for him and I wanted him to feel as though he was making the choices and was being trusted. So for a while he did leave the house but always returned within his time frame. I think the fact that he was afforded some freedom and because it didn't seem to matter to us if he ran or stayed, he did respond. He was a little shocked that we wouldn't follow him and after a time he learned that we trusted him and that was something he had not had in his life before.

The walks became less frequent and eventually ceased, as it was also his test for us. After a settling-in period he would just go out with staff to shop for food or other items and be content with that. It was my thinking that if we did ban his walks he would have snuck out anyway and possibly got himself into trouble so if we showed him a little trust then maybe his mindset would change a little, and it did.

I also outlined some other changes, such as my no swearing rule, and having staff that swore as much as the kids I always knew this was going to be difficult but over time it started to happen and the kids would jokingly take down a staff member if he swore and vice versa. The shirt policy was no black to be worn in the house and this was not that hard to enforce as both boys were to get some nice new T-shirts of their choosing. We saw a lot of white and brighter colours in the house after our shopping day, all without any hate language on them.

I knew I couldn't take their music away from them but we did agree that if they wanted to play their own brand of music they could do so in their own bedrooms but the door must be shut and the volume at a level so that if someone was watching television or listening to house music in the common area, they could do so comfortably. We had a radio which we put on a middle-of-the-road station and that is what everyone listened to. The heavy metal music disappeared very quickly as it was now not annoying to others, which for these kids was part of its purpose; and I am sure it was difficult for them to be isolated in a room all day long listening to that type of music. I would now rarely visit the house and hear anything but the radio or see staff and kids watching television together.

I also had to caution the staff to hold their anger if one of the kids went a little crazy. They were instructed that as long as there was no danger of physical harm to just let the kids go until it had passed and then give them time out and a lot of space to think about what they had done, and then immediately after the incident treat life as normal. Later when the kids were ready, they could take some time to talk about it and let the kids know how it affected them, the staff member, then give them time to tell their story. If the staff could not provide a reason for the behaviour then something else triggered it; what was it?

We had one big incident where one of the kids smashed the television, broke a small table and a few other things but, after that, all others were minor anger outbreaks, which was to be expected. The thing I liked most about that year was when I would come to the house and see a staff member and one of the kids in earnest discussion, like a couple of mates. If I hadn't been seen I would just stay out of sight until they were finished. It was working and the staff, the kids and I were happy. We were constantly asked by the Department of Community Services from the north coast why we were not filing incident reports on the lad they had sent to us and we would truthfully say to them that we had nothing to report. That year and those two young lads gave me a lot of pride and joy but I don't know what became of them—I just hope to this day that they are living a fulfilled and happy life.

Again
To effect change, change the way you see things and people
A little understanding is required

We eventually had to leave Charlton Avenue as the house was sold and although I would never blame one particular event on another, as we still had many more happy times to enjoy, it was also around that time that my marriage to Vicki started to break down. The reasons this occurred should remain personal but what can be said is that I felt as though we were simply drifting apart; maybe not so much for Vicki, but certainly for me. I would in no way ever blame Vicki for our marriage breakdown as I am not sure she even knew it was happening, but I did.

Vicki was a good wife and a wonderful mother and is still a close friend to me and supportive mother to our children. I love and respect Vicki as such, and I am sure we will always remain friends; through our four wonderful children we have a bond that cannot be broken.

I have never really understood how people could love one minute and hate the next as I cannot think of one person that I have given love to that I would not still give love to. It is at times inevitable that someone close to you may hurt you and usually the first thing you ask yourself is why. The trouble is, most people go straight from why to hate, instead of really trying to understand the why. For some, it's just less complicated to hate them, to justify your hurt feelings.

I prefer to dig a little deeper and although my happiness is important to me, the happiness of others I have relationships with outweighs my own personal needs. She would not like to hear this, I know, but if my current wife, Thuy, was to find a more fulfilling happiness with somebody else, although I would feel some sadness, I would also be happy for her; I certainly would not hate her. There are many other forms of betrayal and I have had that in my life too but I certainly don't hate because of it. People who wrong others will live with that guilt and it will be their burden to carry; there is no need for me to carry any hatred as that would just lessen my own personal happiness and wellbeing.

I am not sure that Vicki and I even spoke of separation, it just seemed to happen. I went to work in Sydney and Vicki moved to Newcastle to be close to Maddy; the boys also all eventually ended up in that city. I found a small unit in Sydney and used to visit on weekends but over the course of time those visits became less frequent, until they got to a point where they didn't really occur at all. We were to divorce amicably some nine years later when I met my current wife, Thuy.

Discovering My Aboriginal Culture

I was working in the government's New Enterprise Incentive Scheme in the city of Newcastle, helping to establish small business opportunities for Aboriginal people when the news came through to Mum about her, and our, past. It was a shock for all concerned and my first thought was, *What should I do with this information? Do I just let it be*—as Mum wanted to at the time—*or do I explore more about who I really am and how it will affect my life and those around me?* It was an easy decision for me as I was happy to be one of the First Nations people and to have the blood of those ancestors that dated back some 40,000 years coursing through my veins. I think it was the same for my brother Greg, for if there were to be two Aboriginal kids in our family it was definitely me and Greg. We both had our mother's brown eyes and our skin was a little darker than that of our brothers. So although we all had the blood coursing through us, over time it was both Greg and I who embraced the culture more.

We had many friends on both sides of the divide in our hometown and I was already establishing new friends and acquaintances from Aboriginal communities in Newcastle and the Central Coast through my work and sport. I didn't need to change my lifestyle a great deal; I just had the desire to learn what it truly meant to be an Aboriginal person. Two people who would start me on that pathway were Uncle Jacko, an elder from the Central Coast, and my sister Jenni, also living on the coast. A young lady called Kylie would also play her part in my education as a good and understanding sister who was very much immersed in her culture.

Of course, many people would help educate me—from the cities to outback Australia, everyone I met had an impact in some way on who I am. I am Koori which means I am a blackfella from New South Wales; in Queensland you would be called a Murri and in other states a different term. My mob, which is my tribal group, is called the Kamilaroi and they are located through north/central New South Wales. I would join the Darkinjung Lands Council on the coast as this was where I would be living for the foreseeable future and where I could discover more about the culture and life in general.

Jacko was an activist for Aboriginal rights throughout his life and he taught me much about life as it was and as it is for Aboriginal people in Australia. I also learned a lot in this particular area from a man called Rick Griffith who ran the Mindaribba Local Aboriginal Lands Council in the Maitland area and was also originally from Gunnedah. Jenni was also a very outspoken person on Aboriginal rights and it was from this sister that I was to learn more about the spiritual way.

There are 120 Local Aboriginal Lands Councils (LALCs) throughout New South Wales. Their purpose is to provide a range of services to local Aboriginal people in areas such as housing, legal affairs, employment, training, property acquisition and management and other day-to-day matters relating to members of the LALC.

My work over a period of around ten years saw me meet and work with people in a variety of situations, including juvenile justice centres, prisons, hostels, homecare, employment and training, policing and small business. These employment positions allowed me to meet with elders and community leaders, young entrepreneurs and successful businesspeople from across the nation, as well as those in the entertainment field: actors, singers and traditional performers. I also travelled and met with Aboriginal people from the Northern Territory, Queensland, South Australia and Victoria, each group with their own special traditions and cultural roots.

I was lucky to be placed in these vocations as it gave me access to Aboriginal people from all over Australia and I also gained a broad perspective of what it was like to spend your life as an

Aboriginal person in Australia. Over this period of time I applied for only two positions and was invited to work in another three positions; this was a time of spiritual enlightenment, happiness and also deep sorrow for me.

When it was time for me to leave Australia and venture to Vietnam, I was still not totally fulfilled. Maybe my expectations were too high and my understanding still too limited, but one thing was perfectly clear to me: if you wanted to understand what it was like to be an Aboriginal person in Australia, you needed to be an Aboriginal person.

Don't pretend you know. Don't study and read all of the books and think you know. I am a Black Irishman but if people ask me my nationality, I will always say I am an Aboriginal person from Australia, and I am very proud to say that. There is no halfway pass mark here—you are either fully accepting or not at all. My opportunity to be raised with my extended Aboriginal family was taken away from me by a series of racial government policies and there is nothing I can do to change that. Will I ever truly know what it was and is like to be an Aboriginal person in Australia? No, that was taken away; I can only embrace the little I have.

One thing I really love about the Vietnamese and Aboriginal cultures is that at times you really have no need for names; everyone is referred to as family. When addressing another in Vietnam you would use the terms *Con, Chau, Em, Anh, Chu, Chi, Bac, Co, Ba, Ong*. I am usually referred to as *Anh* (older brother) *Chu* or *Bac* (uncle) or *Ong* (grandfather).

Among Aboriginal people, the terms Bub, Niece, Nephew, Sister, Sis, Brother, Bro, Bruz, Uncle, Auntie, Nan and Pop are used. These are kinship terms usually only used within immediate family in the white community, but in the Aboriginal community they are used more widely throughout communities, extended families and as a sign of respect.

I often think that this is in some part the reason why, over the centuries, Vietnamese, Aboriginal people and other similar groups have been so resilient, for as races they are always together in times of need; they are not a unit of families, they are family.

My pet name for my daughter Maddy has always been 'Bub'. Maddy was still in primary school and I was coaching another of her soccer teams, with a young Aboriginal girl in the team. During a talk with this young girl at training one day, I called her Bub, as in 'niece', as was common in the Aboriginal language; it was the appropriate term for an uncle to use. After training we were heading home when Maddy suddenly burst out crying and I asked her what was wrong and why was she so upset. She replied that it was because I called the other girl Bub and that I should not have because that was her pet name. I had to explain to her why I called the other girl Bub and then tell Maddy that I would never do that again, at least not in her presence—she was and always will be my special Bub.

*****

I love to hear stories of the Dreaming, the time when the ancestor spirits came to the earth in human and animal form and moved through the land, creating the animals, plants, rocks, rivers, mountains and other forms of the land that we know today. Once the ancestor spirits created the world, they transformed into trees, the stars, rocks, watering holes, etc. These are the sacred places of Aboriginal culture and have special meaning.

All of nature has spirit as it was created by spirit. I firmly believe that and love the special relationship indigenous people the world over have with the land and their environment. They were all custodians of the land and its sites and understood the need to nurture and care for it. Unfortunately, now that has largely been taken out of their hands and rather than being guardians of our environment, we can only protest or sit back and watch the destruction of large portions of it due to greed.

The Dreaming never ceases for Aboriginal people; it was then and still is now—there is no word in the hundreds of Aboriginal languages for time. Time refers to the past, present and future but Aboriginal people do not refer to the Dreaming as a time past; in fact it is not a time at all. The legends and stories from the Dreaming are passed down through the generations in storytelling, art and dance. Dreamtime stories can vary between tribes, however, the Rainbow Serpent is one of the few common to all.

In the Dreaming, the world was flat and empty and the Rainbow Serpent lay sleeping under the ground. When it was time, she pushed herself up with all the animals in her belly waiting to be born. Calling to the animals to come from their sleep she threw the land out, making mountains and hills and spilled water over the land, making rivers and lakes. She then made the fire and the sun and all the colours.

The serpent or snake plays an important role for indigenous peoples the world over, for not only does it connect Aboriginal tribes, it also unites people of different cultures and walks of life throughout the world.

A Short Story from the Dreaming: How The White Waratah Became Red *Dharawal People, New South Wales*

The story starts off with two little Wonga pigeons who, when they mate, mate for life and whatever they do they always do it together. If they're building a nest, they build it together. If they're rearing their young, they do that together too.

These two little pigeons decided they wanted to go and gather food one morning; when you see pigeons you never see them sitting up in the trees, eating, you always see them walking around on the ground, picking up things.

So these two little Wonga pigeons were walking around on the ground, picking away as they gathered food and they had a rule never to go out of one another's sight. As they were picking around, the little female looked up and she couldn't see her mate but she didn't take any notice for a little while as she picked around on the ground by herself. She kept looking up every so often and then after a while she started to worry about her mate because there was no sign of him.

So she started calling out and still got no reply. This went on for a little while as she went into the trees, but they also had a rule to never fly up above the canopy of the trees because the hawks would get them, so she just flitted around in the lower branches, calling out to her mate but still got no reply. She got to the stage where she thought 'The only thing I can do now is fly up above the top of the trees and have a look up there'.

As she flew up above the tree tops, sure enough a big hawk grabbed her and clutched her around the breast.

Hawks always have their favourite places to take their food and eat it, so as this big hawk was flying back to his favourite spot to eat this little pigeon, she somehow wriggled and squirmed and broke free of his grip. As she tore away from the hawk her breast tore open and started bleeding.

Because she was wounded she couldn't fly far so she floated down towards the ground; the first thing she landed on was a White Waratah. The blood from her wounds started to turn that White Waratah red.

So she went from White Waratah to White Waratah to White Waratah, and they all became red.

So that little Wonga never found her mate and she eventually died, but that's how the White Waratah became red.

If you go up to a Red Waratah while it's in flower, poke your finger into the flower itself and bring it out—you will get a red stain around your finger. That red stain represents the blood from the pigeon.

I love this story and every time I see a Red Waratah I think of that little Wonga pigeon and how its spirit resides in the flower; it brings a smile to my face and joy to my heart. Do I see that flower differently to you? If you are not a part of the Dreaming, then yes, I guess I do. So many other stories of how nature was created inspire me to view things differently—not just to see a river and think of how beautiful it is but to see that Rainbow Serpent creating the pathway for it to run and the water for it to flow. Everything has spirit and to see it all from an Aboriginal/Dreaming perspective is to enhance the beauty of it all and to feel the spirit within and the energy it creates. I am unsure of how many of my brothers and sisters still feel as I do while living in this modern society but I am sure there are enough of us to keep the Dreaming alive.

I know my sister Jenni feels as I do. One day she asked me to drive her to a spot not too far from the Lands Council offices, as it held special significance for the Darkinjung people. She told me that when we arrived a gentle breeze would arrive to greet us, the ancestral spirits welcoming us and giving us permission to be there. It was as still as any day could get and we were not heading towards the ocean so there would be no sea breeze. When we left the car to walk up this slight incline towards the site, I must admit I was a little sceptical.

We walked through a typical outback-type environment with some small eucalyptus trees, uneven undergrowth and some boulders and rocks scattered around. Jenni said it was once a place where many years past certain Aboriginal rituals and ceremonies were held. True to her word, as we arrived at the site we were greeted by a slight breeze that would rise up and down during our time there. I had no reason to disbelieve anything that she told me as I believed in her as a spirit guide and my teacher. I just stood transfixed to the spot and enjoyed the breeze wrapping around me on this very hot day. I felt consumed with spirit and we said very little during our time there; we just stood or sat and let the moment take us to our own thoughts and feelings.

I was to experience this euphoric feeling many times again, including one very special time at Uluru (Ayers Rock) in Central Australia. I had a couple of days to spare after finishing two months of work in Alice Springs. During my time in Alice I witnessed many things that seemed to me to reflect a time that existed possibly 100 years ago. The treatment of the Aboriginal community was deplorable and to me the town was just a racist frontier town, a step back in time. All I could see were white people making money off black people in various forms, yet treating them as rubbish in the streets. Again, this was a first perception, but it was one that changed little during my time there as I tried to understand why. If I put all of that aside, I would remember the beauty of the country and those moments when I connected with the local people in a spiritual manner and also hearing many stories about the Dreaming and how their landscape was shaped.

The most surreal moment for me was visiting a local hospital and witnessing a person translating an Aboriginal language into English. It turned out that the person needing the translation was a lady who had danced in the opening ceremony of the Sydney Olympics in 2000. She came from a community around 200 kilometres south-west of Alice and like many others in her community she did not speak English. They lived much the same as their ancestors had and after witnessing the treatment of the people in the town and many other places throughout Australia, it was comforting for me to know that up in these vast desert lands people still retained their culture, their language and their pride.

I flew to Uluru with my boss Russell; this was my first time there. I was really happy as it was such a beautiful place to visit and for me another spiritual journey. I thought that Uluru itself was spectacular as we drove around it; we stopped to view it but we did not climb the rock as Uluru is a sacred site to the Anangu people and we had to show respect to those people and not invade one of their sacred sites without their permission. It is heartening to know that the rock is now banned to all climbing activities. Numbers had declined markedly over the years until only approximately 16% of all tourists coming to the area climbed Uluru after a special education program was put in place about its cultural significance.

Uluru was created by ten ancestral beings, with each having a part in the creation of the rock. The southern area of Uluru formed due to a war between the poisonous snakes and the carpet snakes. The north-west side of Uluru formed from the hare people, otherwise known as Mala. The Indigenous community regard Uluru as a living form and it is especially sacred to the

Yankunytjatjara and Pitjantjatjara people. They consider this structure a dwelling for past spirits to live in.

My next spiritual experience took place in another outcrop of rocks nearby, a very special place known as Kata Tjuta, around forty kilometres from Uluru. There is a group of thirty-six large ancient rock formations believed to have been formed 500 million years ago; the words Kata Tjuta come from the Pitjantjatjara Aboriginal word meaning 'many heads'.

One legend depicts the Kata Tjuta as the home of the giant snake called Wonambi, the Dreamtime figure responsible for the formation of gullies, rivers and billabongs in Central Australia. According to legends, Wonambi stays curled up in a waterhole in the highest peak during the rainy season and crawls down to the gorge during the dry season. The dark lines on the side of the rocks are believed to be his beard, and the wind that blows through the gorge, his breath—gentle breezes on some days, huge hurricanes when he's angry.

I guess we found Wonambi in a peaceful mood that day as we walked around the formations, again on another still day. There was one particular gorge that we walked to and it was there that I could feel the gentle breath of Wonambi; not different in any way at all to the day with Jenni on the coast, but welcoming and spiritual. Again, I was taken to another time and space.

That night we stayed in a rented tent but not just any old tent—it was quite luxurious for a tent, with two beds and electricity. Russell and I spent most of the night outside on a couple of chairs at a small table, eating a meal, him drinking beer, me coffee and then tea. It was an ideal place to talk and really get to know the person you were with. There is no pollution in the central desert and we were presented with a night sky I will never forget, with everything so clear and so big. The stars were like little moons and the moon, well, it was just bigger and brighter. The peace afforded us on that night is hard to explain; not something to be talked of but something that needs to be experienced.

I have often thought about what life would be like without the buildings, houses, structures, the invasion—it must have been so idyllic for the First Nations people but it is also something that need not be completely lost. When I left the coast and lived and worked in the hustle and bustle of Sydney, I still sought nature. Occasionally at lunchtimes or after work I would go to Hyde Park or a smaller park near our inner city offices and find the oldest tree I could. I would remove my shoes and socks, lean back against that old tree, place the soles of my feet firmly on the grass, close my eyes and just leave it all behind.

Parents and Parenting

Before I left the coast to live and work in Sydney, another sad event would take place—the passing of my father. As mentioned earlier, my father was a hard man; he was not someone you could sit and have an emotional life story moment with, and not someone you would hug and say, 'I love you'. Times have changed and people's ways have changed, and it makes me happy that I do have those moments with my own sons and daughter. I don't know why but I had a feeling that my father's time was coming to a close and there were things I wanted to tell him but I knew that I could not say them to him in person. I was also not sure if I would see him again; we did not return home very often as we had a busy life with the kids on the coast. I wrote him a letter and the short version of it was that I told him that no matter what occurred in our house during my childhood and no matter what personal clashes we had, I wanted him to know that I loved and respected him as my father and I just wanted to take this time to thank him for all that he had done for me.

I didn't get to see him again but Mum told me what a surprise he got when he received the letter and that he cried when reading it—the first time she had ever seen him cry. She said that he was so happy and wanted to show it to everyone who visited. That, in turn, made me cry as I was happy that the letter had touched him in such a way and I hoped that at the end it made his passing a little easier.

Parenting is not an easy thing to do, but it is most certainly very rewarding to watch your children grow into adulthood and know that you had a role to play in how each child adapts to life. There were lots of ups and downs while my kids were growing up but it is how you deal with those events when they happen that define you, not the events themselves.

When their teenage years came I knew full well that I was raising four individuals and each personality needed to be approached in a different manner. If there are certain things you don't want your kids to do in life, then as I said before, be sure you are the example: 'do as I do', not 'don't do as I did'. Although that lesson came a little late to me in life, it came at the right time, when they were maturing from young teenagers to adults. I knew at that time I was living my life and making decisions the way they were meant to be and that this was closer to the real me than anything that had gone before.

I never gave my kids the material things in life that many others had but they also did not miss out on much. We had each other and as we grew as a family; so too did our love and respect for each other. From love comes happiness and when all is said and done, that is what everyone seeks. For each individual it may come in different forms and that is something that needs to be understood as a parent. My way may not be the way of my children but if they can understand and respect my way then I am happy, and I need to reciprocate that understanding. My role has been to guide, to give advice when needed or asked for, and not to impose my beliefs upon them but to let them grow as individuals and to make their own mistakes that they will learn from. Parenting finishes when you die, so be prepared for the long haul.

Sydney

After some years of employment in Sydney and a regular daily commute from the Central Coast I returned to live in the city some 35 years after I originally left my hometown as a 15-year-old to explore life and to see what it held for me. The journey to date had been enlightening in many different ways and this journey would also provide many more elements to my continual growth. I lived in the suburb of Petersham, a multicultural suburb of Sydney well known for its famous Portuguese chicken. That delicious chicken brought people on the weekends from far and wide to feast on it and other Portuguese delights, usually pastries. I had only four train stops into the centre of the city for my work, and two in the other direction to Ashfield, with its wonderful Chinese food and large shopping centre.

I had a small flat and over time made it comfortable to suit me. I purchased a Chinese cookbook and if I didn't eat out I was cooking and eating Chinese food. I was not and still am not a very good cook. The cookbook usually had recipes to feed two to four people; I could have broken the recipes down to suit one but I would usually just cook what was recommended and eat the same dish a couple of nights in a row. It was easy to arrive home and microwave something from the night before and the dishes always contained a good quantity of vegetables so in a sense it was healthy eating—well, that's my take on it anyway.

Prior to leaving for Vietnam I worked for the New South Wales Ombudsman's Office, and did so happily. All the staff, from the ombudsman himself down were all very friendly, dedicated and grounded people. It was important work and extremely rewarding.

For those who are unsure of an ombudsman's role, in its simplest form the Ombudsman's Office deals with complaints about public sector agencies, local councils, community service providers, employment-related child protection, custodial centres and public interest disclosures. The ombudsman reports the findings to a special parliamentary committee; the office cannot prosecute agencies or individuals but makes recommendations to the lead agency to help resolve matters.

My work with the Aboriginal unit primarily involved the custodial sector and working with Aboriginal agencies to provide better outcomes for their communities. One such initiative was to investigate child sexual assault in rural and remote Aboriginal communities.

My humanity at times would be tested by this work and would also show my frailties. Interviewing in the prison system was not an easy task but it is the right of everyone within this system to lodge complaints with a neutral body regarding basic human rights. The system really has only two options: to either execute extreme offenders or house them. Australia does not have the death penalty, therefore they house all criminals, and in doing so, all still have basic human rights. People have different views on matters like this but I cannot support a death penalty and I believe the majority of my fellow citizens feel the same.

As we were at the prisons to interview detainees about their basic human rights and quite often the behaviours of the prison employees towards them, we never really felt welcome at any prison or juvenile justice centre. To some degree, we were seen as the enemy and when there we would get that feeling from most within the system. We always thought that if a riot were to break out, we would not be very high on the priority list for rescue.

We had movement restrictions placed upon us for our own safety; these were tightened or given some liberty depending upon the status of the facility. One such place we were very happy to see such tight security was at the Supermax facility in Goulburn. The Supermax houses the majority of New South Wales and Australia's most notorious and dangerous prisoners; it is a detention centre that sits within but is separate from a maximum security prison.

We had interviewed some inmates within the maximum security prison and we had one inmate to interview in Supermax. The process to get into the facility was obviously very stringent and as with all interviews here and in the other prisons we visited, we did not know the prisoner's name or his crimes. The prisoners here spend sixteen hours a day in their cells and other hours in a small exercise area attached to their cell. For most there was no communication at all with other inmates, although some who had good behaviour were given the opportunity to communicate for a couple of hours a day with just one other prisoner.

The prisoner we were to interview was brought to our interview room and this in itself was surreal if you have never been in this type of environment before. He was shackled around the wrists with a long chain running from those cuffs to more around his ankles so that he could only shuffle along. As he came towards us for the interview he was sandwiched in the middle of four prison guards. We could only sit and wonder what he did to deserve this—it was best we didn't know.

Later, in another maximum security prison, things went slightly amiss for us while interviewing an inmate who gave us information that we did not want or need to know. The reason we are not to know the crimes of inmates is to ensure there will be no bias in our reporting, but on this occasion it would unfold. As we were conducting the interview the prisoner started to reveal who he was, what he was convicted of and also the crimes of which he claimed his innocence. We repeatedly told him that we were not to have this information and he should speak to his lawyer regarding these matters, not us. He was a convicted paedophile, something we already knew as his conviction was very high profile. It was something we would never address at interview, but he proceeded to do just that.

After he acknowledged the procedure we needed to adopt, we heard his complaint; even if I wanted to recall it I don't believe I could, for at the time I questioned my humanity and also any fair hearing his complaint may get from me. I firmly believe, like most in our community, that any crime against innocent children is the most heinous crime one could commit and I struggled to remain impartial.

We treated his complaint in line with our guidelines and it formed part of our report but for a time in that interview it was all a blur for me; a time when you are carrying out the task in front of you but not really aware of it, the mind is elsewhere. My feeling was of sadness for the victims and although I had a job to do, I also had a strong urge to leave the room. That was one time I honestly didn't care about the complaint I was hearing because for a time the gravity of the crimes overwhelmed my resolve.

Some visits had their lighter moments, such as in the minimum security prisons. The majority of offenders within the prison system are repeat offenders and you find many of them in minimum security, both male and female, who are released but find that life is too difficult for them on the outside so they commit a minor crime just to come back into the system. Friendship groups are usually formed through families and others with whom you have common interests, and that is also the case with criminals, as they cannot adapt to the formalities and rigours of life outside and are more comfortable with those of the same ilk.

Juvenile justice centres were completely different and although they too, at times, had a high level of security they were a much more relaxed, though sometimes rowdy, place to visit. These were kids who were in the centres largely because of the environment in which they'd been raised as well as the abuse they had to try and cope with as children. Most were a little rebellious and would let us know that as we passed by or they would be completely withdrawn, deeply depressed and medicated in such a way that they resembled zombies.

Having worked with kids back home with Father Shanahan and with the youth care group on the coast I could really sympathise with these kids; although it was not our job to counsel them I did hope in some way that the work we did would benefit them a little. Most were repeat offenders and many confided in us that this was the only place they felt safe so when released they would find a way to get back. Unfortunately for most it would later in life lead to time in the adult prison, where the cycle would begin again.

If a child or a young adult cannot find some personal sort of intervention, or if they don't accept help, it creates a vicious cycle that over time becomes increasingly difficult to escape. The relevant authorities try hard but they are under-resourced and the type of one-on-one counselling that is required for these kids just cannot be in this system. They need mentors, but unfortunately the people who are closest to them, the guards and social workers, spend much of their time in anger trying to cope with the collective behaviours of so many. Some will find life too hard and leave it by their own hand, others will just continually go through the systems. But there are always a few who will escape the blackness for the light and they are the ones who can, with the proper training, become great counsellors themselves or very good mentors for the youth in their own local communities.

The poem below was written by Christine, a sixteen-year-old Aboriginal girl in Yasmar Detention Centre. I was given it approximately 15 years ago and I had it laminated and carry it with me everywhere I live. It has been my constant companion, just like the book I carry, Zen Bones–Zen Flesh *and another book,* Last Night I Dreamt of Peace. *That book is the story of Dang Thuy Tram a young Vietnamese doctor during the American War. Thuy Tram was a true heroine and the book is an account of the war from the Vietnamese side, about an innocent young woman just out of university and the impact the war had on her, written in her personal diary. The Zen book provides me with answers to life's riddles while the story of Tram gives me the desire to help and to better understand. The poem from Christine reminds me that no matter what occurs in my life it will never take me to a place as dark and deep as the one Christine was living in at that time. I hope she found the light and is leading a fulfilling life. I may never know but I prefer to think that rather than the alternative she spoke of. I thank her for expressing her feelings and opening mine; this poem may have been the turning point for her, it was one of many for me.*

Overload
Continual darkness on the road to nowhere,
The isolating experience, the unbearable despair.
Exploding sensation inside my head;
Wanting to die, in a way already dead.
Relying on drugs for some kind of high;
Afraid to live and afraid to die!
Guts knotted up and mind still a mess
I continue to fight but it seems useless.
Try to be the right person and do the right thing...
What are the consequences, what does it bring?
Get rid of the cut up feeling inside;
If I can't stay cool, I'll just run and hide.
I look in the mirror at the ugliness staring back;
Got to keep running, here's a person you can't back!
Avoiding myself, hiding away...
It's so hard to do, day after day.
I can't afford to stop and think...
I black out, have another drink.
I keep doing this, where will it end—
In an asylum, around the bend?
Achieving that doesn't have much gain...
I JUST WANT SOMEONE TO TAKE AWAY MY PAIN

There would be many more moments at work that I had to release as quickly as I could, and others that I wanted to retain that would lead me to be the person I am today—neither good nor bad, just Terry Donnelly. It was during this time in Sydney that I really enhanced my spiritual happiness and learned that I was comfortable with who I was and how I was leading my life. Being alone can be a blessing, a time of discovery.

On a daily basis I try to abide by my pathway to peace; if I slip I return.

If you are still searching, set yourself a good moral and ethical compass like the pathway below and simply live your life in good conduct. Then you will have the happiness and peace you need.

My Pathway to Peace

Do one thing at a time, do it slowly and deliberately
Do it completely
Put space between things
Designate time for things you enjoy
Take time to sit
Smile and always try to help others
Let daily chores become meditation
Don't think too much, do it
Act on things you can control, do not [be] concern[ed]
with things you cannot
Think before you speak, then speak slowly and deliberately
Live simply—always be humble

Zet

Sydney was also a blessing if you were a food lover, with so many different suburbs specialising in certain types of foods, usually dependent upon the backgrounds of the local population. The city itself was like a big smorgasbord with so many restaurants and food courts catering to a variety of different tastes. If you went to one of the large food courts in the city you could find food from the world over and it was in such a food court that my life would take a drastic turn.

I left the office for lunch one day and went to the food court on the ground floor of our building; although I had my favourites I wanted to try something different. That was when I noticed a Vietnamese eatery and sampled for the first time the traditional noodle soup of Vietnam called *pho* (sounds like 'fur'). I loved it then, as I do now, and any time I feel a little off-colour, or have a cold or flu, I will head out to my favourite *pho* shop in Hanoi to eat. To me it not only tastes great but also has some medicinal value. Add some lime juice, a little chili sauce and heaven awaits you.

I visited this particular shop on many occasions sampling other dishes, and over time I struck up a relationship with the owners.

They occasionally gave me a free meal or extra portions, as did my friends at the Portuguese chicken shop in Petersham; maybe they liked me or maybe I just looked really poor, or—more likely—they were just very generous people.

Over the period of time I frequented the shop we talked quite a lot about Vietnam and in particular about an orphanage in Ho Chi Minh City (Saigon) that they thought I should visit. It took some time but eventually we arranged for that to happen; prior to my departure the owners' young daughter Linh would meet me at the food court for around 30 minutes each Friday afternoon and give me some basic Vietnamese lessons. It was through this chance meeting and this wonderful bowl of *pho* that the next adventure in my life would begin, though at the time I had no idea of the magnitude of that change.

First Visit to Vietnam

I arranged my annual holidays and within a few months found myself standing in Tan Son Nhat International Airport arrivals in Ho Chi Minh City, staring out among the mass of people in front of me and looking for my name on one of the many signboards being held up by taxi drivers and guides.

It was all very daunting for me for, although I had travelled extensively throughout my own country, I had never been overseas and was immediately taken aback by the sheer volume of people in front of me and the heat and humidity that hit me like a hammer as soon as I stepped outside the terminal doors. I found my name and met with Tuyen, a friend of the orphanage who did a lot of fundraising for them; she would be my main guide on this trip and one of the very few people I encountered who spoke English.

We took a taxi to the apartment that had been arranged for me in District 3, which was some distance from the main tourist area of Saigon and an area that contained very few foreigners. During this trip the only interaction I had was with Vietnamese people. The trip to the apartment was something of a culture shock in a city with around 12 million residents, and with cars, buses, trucks and literally thousands of motorbikes trying to share the road, it seemed that all of them were beeping their horns. It was evening peak hour and a very slow journey as we seemed to just move from one traffic jam to the next.

When we arrived at the apartment I was tired from the flight and still in a little shock from the volume of traffic and people on the roads; it was chaos but somehow it worked. The apartment was quite comfortable but we were not too far from the main thoroughfare into the city centre. As the night wore on it appeared the traffic would never let up, all I could hear were the sounds of horns blaring—this was not in an aggressive manner, just people letting others know that they were there or that they were coming through. It appeared at that time—and still does today—that although there *are* road rules, not many people seem to follow them. You also learn not to make great use of rearview mirrors as the accident is never behind you, it is always in front, or could come from any sideways direction.

The next day I asked if I could be moved to a room at the back of the building to avoid another sleepless night and early morning wake-up, courtesy of the traffic on the main road. I learned that most people in Vietnam go to bed early and rise very early in the mornings. Tuyen met me the next morning and rather than go directly to the orphanage she showed me around the local area a little, to introduce me to authentic Vietnamese food and show me some places I could eat. The next day she showed me the best way to get to the orphanage, this involved a local bus and then a short tuk tuk ride, in distance about ten kilometres from the apartment.

The orphanage was started by a wonderful but very firm lady called Chi Cu who ran the orphanage with the help of her six sisters. The sisters also manufactured clothing from their house to sell overseas. Chi Cu used to work at a local hospital as a nurse and one day rescued an abandoned baby and took her back to her home. Occasionally some young women who found themselves pregnant and knowing that because of their particular life circumstances they would not be able to care for a child they would abandon them at the hospital and run away, I am sure with much heartbreak.

Over time Chi Cu would build on the number of babies and also accepted young children from stricken and poor families unable to give their children proper care. If you are poor in Vietnam it is very difficult to get by and by giving up their children to an orphanage, the parents would hope that the child may have a better chance in life and that they themselves would have time to find work to just survive. With help from family, friends and eventually different sponsors and support groups, Chi Cu was able to extend her house and at the time of my visit had fifty-two children in her care.

She was a compassionate and caring woman, as were the other members of her family, but she also ruled with an iron fist; while the children loved her, they also knew any transgressions would be met with strict discipline. I recall one day there were around twelve kids in an outside area where they should not have been and as Chi Cu rounded them up to come back inside they had to pass by her and she took her cane and gave each a tap on the backside as they entered the house. It seemed the older they were the harder the tap. I didn't react in any way as it was not my place and I was just seeing what was classed as a normal event back in my childhood. I quickly understood that yes, I was back in another time and yes, I needed to recognise that and not try to impose my Western ideals.

I gave some English lessons to the older kids, planned some activities and games and just helped out in general where I could. Chi Cu had a simple philosophy on how volunteers at the centre should work: "If you see something that needs doing, just do it—no need to ask me." I also visited the disability centre next door and learned from those men how to appreciate life no matter how bad the hardship. They made a little extra money by making stuffed toys that would subsidise the shelter and food provided for them at the centre. Life in my perception seemed very difficult for them but each time I visited I would find them smiling and laughing as a group and generally enjoying the little they had.

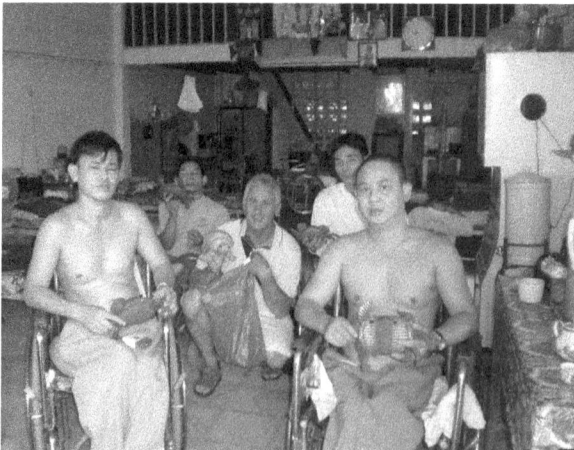

On this trip I saw another side of life: a different culture, traditions that are still followed, a different mindset to life, and I met some of the most generous people I have ever known. They changed my way of viewing and living life forever.

Vietnam is a highly polluted place, especially in the cities, with smoke and gases from factories, waste polluting almost all the waterways, dirty streets creating dust in the air from seemingly never-ending construction and the trucks from those construction sites continually spilling dirt on the roads. Vietnam also has caring and loving people, the majority with the Buddhist philosophy on life, strong family connections for both past and present members, and a pride people carry in their hearts for their country. Life can be lived at a leisurely pace and nothing should be rushed; do what you need to do when you have to but then let it go and live life.

There were two particular events that made me feel very humble and along with other future interactions gave me a true love of this country.

I did a little weekend travelling on this trip and one of those journeys took me on a short road trip to the city of Can Tho, which is south of Saigon and lies on the mighty Mekong River. Here, I hired a small boat that would take me along the main river and also into some of the many tributaries that ran off the Mekong. The boat was operated by a man called Ha and his wife Thuong and this was their only source of income. The boat didn't belong to them, so along with the hire fee for the boat and having to pay for fuel, they were left with very little income even when they were lucky enough to have a busy day with tourists and the deliveries they made around the river.

I had Tuyen and two other friends of hers with me and we had a great day exploring the waterways, visiting the floating markets and stopping to eat a chicken lunch on one of the small islands on this great river. After the tour Ha invited me to dinner at his place and arranged to pick me up at the waterway not too far from my hotel; he lived across the river on what could be said was the poorer side of Can Tho.

Their house was a very small mudbrick home that had one living area and a private bathroom/toilet area. Both Ha and Thuong, along with their two children and Ha's mother, slept in the living area that was also the kitchen and lounge area. They served a simple meal that was within their means and as I was their guest they made sure that I ate the more generous and tasty portions. After dinner we walked around the area and stopped occasionally to sit and drink tea with other family members and friends who lived nearby. There was nothing spectacular about the area and there were no sights to see that would be unforgettable but it was one of the most pleasant evenings of my life, shared with a very kind and loving family. It was an evening I carry with me, always.

The next evening I invited the family to come over to the hotel and to share a meal at a restaurant that I invited them to select; once again we had an enjoyable night. It was very special for the kids as it was the first time they had been to a restaurant and it was also the first time in the fourteen years since their marriage that Ha and Thuong had eaten out. We said our farewells that night as I was to leave for Saigon the next morning but just as the bus for Saigon arrived in the morning so did the family and we sadly said goodbye again. This family left an indelible mark in my heart and again drew me closer to Vietnam. We maintained contact for a short time but I have not ventured south again, as yet.

Another memorable encounter from that trip occurred when I was walking back to the apartment one night after a day at the orphanage. An older man was sitting outside his house drinking tea and trying to cool down in the heat and as I walked by, he motioned for me to stop and drink with him, which I was very happy to do—later I would find out that this was a common occurrence here. He had a couple of small chairs and a table and he prepared a cup and poured some tea; it was one cup of many to come for if I motioned to leave he would stop me and pour another. We had no common language but he did ask me where I was from and I understood that, for along with "How old are you?", it was a common phrase asked of foreigners. I replied, "Uc", which in Vietnamese is 'Australia'. He also motioned about the American War and I understood enough to know that he had fought in it.

We really didn't communicate about anything else, we just sat and drank tea, watching the world pass by with our only interruptions being some members of the family coming out to refresh the tea and bring some snacks. I sat for maybe an hour and we said nothing else to each other, but on parting it was again as though I was leaving a member of the family. I thanked him as best I could in my broken Vietnamese for the tea and if I could have I would have thanked him for his kindness and willingness to share with me; not only his tea but also that space in time that I really enjoyed. We need to treasure these moments of kindness; occasionally no words are required and sometimes life is better like that. Maybe my silent days were a preparation for this.

I Have nothing to say, I wish I knew more people like that
Zet

My time in Vietnam was coming to an end but there were two things certain as a result of this trip: one was that I would return to Australia forever changed as a result of the people that I had met and the interactions we had; and two was that I would one day return. Exactly how or when that would occur I was uncertain but Vietnam and its people had touched me in such a way that it was inevitable.

Return to Sydney

I had four weeks of holiday leave but spoke to my then boss Julianna and asked if I could extend an extra week without pay; Julianna, being a generous and kind person, agreed. It was sad to leave everyone at the orphanage but they, like me, knew I would return one day and the kids were used to people coming and going. I was happy in the knowledge that one day we would meet again. Leaving Vietnam was difficult but it had given me a completely different perspective on life and how I could and should live.

I returned to work and my little flat in Petersham, still the man who had left but now changed in ways that were deep in my heart. I would spend more time meditating in a manner not considered the traditional way, but the Terry way. It is generally regarded that sitting cross-legged in the lotus position is the correct way to meditate, but there is no correct way; meditation can take many forms, from gurus across the world sitting for days in very awkward positions, to open-eye meditation, walking meditation, meditation during chores or even my form of meditation of lying on my back in the ocean. No matter how you meditate, just be sure you are comfortable as the only goal of meditation is to reach nothingness, no thing; to free yourself completely from the stresses of life and to return to that life completely relaxed. Meditation for me slows everything—my heart, my mind, my thoughts, my reactions. I do so in a variety of ways and use a variety of methods.

The attainment of nothingness is not easily done as it is not easy to completely still the mind. So if nothingness is not valid then the next best thing is to focus on only one particular point. You will see many people and monks using things such as candles, a crack in the wall, a small object or even a single flower. This is oneness, where you become one with that particular focus point and there is nothing else—your mind is completely free of all other distractions.

When I believed that I had reached nothingness during meditation it was like a sleep, just darkness but no dreams, no thoughts. I guess it is quite possible that it was sleep, but still, it was nothing and I would always come back totally relaxed. Meditation times would vary, sometimes ten minutes, sometimes one hour. Just a few minutes of closing your eyes and blocking out all sensory thoughts and objects can really slow and relax the mind; there is no time limit imposed, it just really depends on you.

Other times if I had something on my mind, like a question or situation to which I was having trouble finding an answer, I would go to one specific place to find that answer. I am unsure how the location and means of finding the answer came about but after the first time it stayed with me and provided guidance when needed— my secret place. I would begin to meditate but not to achieve nothingness; I would go to what seemed to me to be an island in a tropical location. It would begin with me walking through what was quite a dense jungle but with a wide pathway through the jungle littered with dry leaves from the overhanging trees; I would always feel them crunching under my steps.

The pathway led to a small pool located in a sandstone outcrop and I would always first swim in the pool and then lie on the sandstone and feel the warmth of the sunshine penetrate my body. When I was totally relaxed I would rise and walk to a small waterfall close by. There were two sitting rocks, one on either side of the falls. I would sit on one and on the other side was a small Buddha, always the same—he looked like a small happy Buddha. We would sit a while and then I would ask him the question that was on my mind and he would always give me the same reply—no reply. He would turn his head towards me, stare a little in displeasure and then turn away. It was like he wanted to give me a Buddha slap that was sometimes used by monks on stubborn students trying to find enlightenment. Some students would struggle for a long period of time to find an answer to a particular koan that would satisfy the monk but with the sudden shock of a slap across the face from the monk it would appear to them and thus, enlightenment. So it was with me and this little Buddha; and he was right all the time, there was no need for him to waste his breath as I already knew the answer—it was always with me, I just needed to think less.

I do the same with staff and friends when they ask me a question to something I feel they already know or they need to work out themselves. I just look at them and then look away, maybe threaten them with a Buddha slap (in Vietnamese it is called *Phat Tat*). They will then wander off and think about their question, arrive at the answer and move on.

As I said, meditation can come in many forms: there's no right, no wrong, do it your way. I also sometimes gravitated to the night sky and ran pure energy through my body by utilising my third eye (another story, another time). I mentioned that it was only four stops from the train station near my home to the city centre where I worked and this became another medium for meditation and the transference of love; a little more challenging because of the clutter of people and noises associated with the train.

I would stand in between two seating compartments, near the entrance to the carriage, lean against the wall, close my eyes and feel love. How I do that is to feel the energy within me and see it as bright illumination, thousands upon thousands of particles of energy matter. I would create a bubble around me and in the middle of all the clutter of people going about their daily business and the noise of the train I would feel totally at ease and full of wonderment. Before my stop arrived I would transfer this love through all the carriages of the train; inside my mind I could see the carriages illuminated and then again in my mind I would wish everyone on the train love in their lives and happiness throughout the day ahead. I would leave the train refreshed and happy.

As I said, my way is definitely my way. I would not be a good teacher of meditation but my way always brings me happiness and serenity, in a very weird kind of way. Find your own way and don't get too caught up in the proper way, it doesn't exist. Sometimes it's good to be a little not so normal (ok, a little crazy). I once attended a meditation session with 200 other people in Hanoi. An older man asked the monk who was delivering the teaching if it was necessary to sit crossed-legged when meditating as his knees were not good and it caused him pain. The monk replied that you can meditate in any fashion that you like as long as you are comfortable and the goal is the same; he then proceeded to demonstrate walking meditation.

I also try and do at least one good deed a day—something to change somebody's life a little, something that will bring a smile to their face, for if they are smiling you know they are feeling a good emotion inside. Near my work there was a lady who sold flowers out of a little booth on the street. She was there well before I would arrive and, I imagine, late into the night. I had never bought flowers from her but I had wondered if things were ever reversed for her—did anybody buy her flowers? So one day I did. I bought a bunch of roses from her and after paying for them, I gave them back to her. She asked if something was wrong and I told her my reason for doing that and that the flowers were a gift from me to her. She smiled and we both had a bit of a laugh and she seemed very grateful for the gesture. I am not sure what happened to the flowers, obviously something that she did not have a great need for but I hoped they would find their way to her home. It didn't really matter as her smile and our brief moment together were enough.

I would also sometimes buy coffee for homeless guys on the street and sit and have a chat. I actually got a donation from somebody going by one day; he kept walking but turned his head and we smiled about his deed. People on the streets have different reasons for being there and I always enjoyed hearing their stories. Although sometimes very sad for me and for them, this moment was just about the time somebody actually sat and listened to their stories, when somebody took the time to show they cared.

I returned to Vietnam and the orphanage the following year during my holidays and once again had a wonderful journey. I spent a lot of time with the kids and Chi Cu and her family. I travelled a little to towns I had not been before, welcomed new friends into my life and understood the culture a little more. Vietnam is a developing country and I think sometimes tourists don't really understand what that means, and go with their expectations raised far too high. Even on the trail specifically tailored for tourists most things are way below the standard of Western countries. I am sure if more people understood they would complain less but for some, unfortunately, that is just their nature. Although a developing country, Vietnam also has issues of its own with 92 million people living on a relatively small piece of land, so growth will take time. Nothing on this trip had changed my desire to live in Vietnam, if anything it was enhanced and I knew the time was just coming a little closer.

My work at the Ombudsman's Office continued, with the most difficult assignment I was to have still in front of me. It is unfortunate that in this world, no matter race or religion, there are still perpetrators among us who abuse the rights of children; the most despicable of these people are those who sexually abuse an innocent child. Although this vile practice unfortunately occurs throughout all communities in Australia and around the world, it was my task as part of the Aboriginal unit at the office to investigate the extent of it in Aboriginal communities and then it would be for the office to make recommendations to the relevant parties on how to try to put an end to it.

We were reasonably intelligent individuals so we knew that no matter what we found we would not be able to stop it. But we hoped that in some small way we would be able to lessen it and find a way to counsel and protect the children who are the victims of these crimes. My time working with the young people on the Central Coast who had been through this had shown me the damage this could do to a child's mind. So if we couldn't stop it, how could we better educate society about the signs it may be occurring in their neighbourhood or family and what resources could we use to best find a way for the kids and others to come forward?

Along with my colleague and little sister Kylie, we travelled for two weeks throughout rural and remote areas of New South Wales conducting public forums on the matter. We knew from the start it would be a difficult and emotional assignment but we never really envisioned exactly how hard it would be. Each forum, no matter the size, was much the same: accusations, stories from women in the communities who had been subjected to this as a child, stories of it currently happening, denials that it existed at all from other members, crying, arguing and sometimes just a general melee.

It was hard to take control of the meeting at times, given the subject matter and we knew it was always going to be an intense atmosphere; there were times we didn't want to control it as we knew that some people needed the release. There were matters that we could report and others that would need to go through the local police but being such small communities that was always difficult, for when we left, the people who lived in these communities still had to live there. Although we thought we had heard enough, we knew we had not heard it all.

Given the distance between towns we would normally only have one meeting a day but occasionally there were two. By the end of the first week we were happy to have some downtime. It was difficult to attend these forums and then write them up each night and do exactly the same the next day. We had a weekend to relax in one of the major rural centres, a town called Dubbo. Kylie had her boyfriend come to visit for the weekend so I didn't see too much of her and I just spent my time walking around Dubbo, trying to relax at coffee shops, local eateries and seeing some sights. I also did some meditation to try to clear my head but the following week was never far from my mind.

The next week went much the same as the first, with nothing really changing at the meetings and we were getting more tired and emotionally drained as the week rolled on. It was Friday morning and we were feeling the effects of a mentally tough two weeks but we had one more meeting to attend in the town of Dunedoo before driving back to Dubbo and taking a flight to Sydney. I admit saying to Kylie that I really hoped no one would turn up at the meeting and when we arrived at the meeting hall there was actually nobody there. The hall was locked and we thought we might get our wish, but somebody did arrive and open the hall and slowly people came in. It was a feeling of relief when we finished the meeting and of some joy when we arrived back in Sydney. I had a quiet weekend in my little flat; it was like a safe haven for me and I always felt secure and comfortable there. Although I meditated and released, the past two weeks were still there hidden in a little recess of my mind.

I went to work on the Monday to find that Kylie had taken a flex day, so I caught up on some other work and started compiling my part of the report. Early in the afternoon Julianna called me into her office and asked me what was wrong. I was a little puzzled as I thought everything was fine but she told me that I was being a little short with some members of staff and that they could feel that something wasn't right with me. I was always a relaxed and happy individual around the office so I had to think about how I had changed or why others thought this. I sat there in silence for a moment and the next thing I knew, I burst into tears and all of the pent-up emotion of the past two weeks just left my body.

I was grateful to the staff for noticing a difference that I was personally unaware of and also very happy to have such a thoughtful and caring boss. Yes, grown men do cry and it was exactly what was needed; sometimes you just don't realise the burden you are carrying until your actions give you away and when the release comes, no matter what form, the burden dissipates. So it was with me but my immediate thoughts turned to Kylie and if I was feeling this way then how was she? I made a phone call to check on her and she told me that she had released over the weekend with her mum in much the same way as I had today, and that she too was now fine. So that venture was over and I prepared for my next trip to Vietnam.

Time Out to Meet With an Elders Group and Embracing Outback (New South Wales)

Hanoi

This time I took two months leave-without-pay and headed to Hanoi in Northern Vietnam to work with a soon-to-be lifelong friend, Jimmy Pham, who runs a very good hospitality training company for street kids (KOTO is the name of his organisation: Know One – Teach One). I would again have a great time meeting some wonderful kids in the program who were later to become lifelong friends, and there was also time to admire the work that Jimmy and his staff do by giving these kids an opportunity in life they would otherwise not have.

Hanoi is the capital city of Vietnam and the political hub, while Saigon is more of a commercial/economic-driven city and is far more Westernised than its northern partner, Hanoi. Unfortunately, Westernisation always seems to bring with it the seedy side and Saigon has a far greater crime rate and drug use rate than Hanoi and is a very busy city. Hanoi of course is also busy, but to me more relaxed and easy-going, and a far more traditional atmosphere than Saigon. Hanoi also enjoys a small window of winter, spring and autumn so it is pleasant after a really hot summer to have a little respite from the heat. Saigon is hot, hot, hot, with dry and rainy seasons.

I saw some of the beautiful sights of the north such as Halong Bay and Sapa, and I visited some other regional locations and ancient pagodas to satisfy my Buddhist leanings. I again enjoyed the company of its peoples and their way of life, the primary reasons I love this country so much.

When I did return to live in Vietnam I spent some time living in Saigon, Dalat, Sapa and Hanoi but I always knew that Hanoi was where I would settle. I do have a favourite city, one where I lived for six months, and that is Dalat, located in the central Vietnam highlands. It is a truly beautiful small city with an ideal climate all year round. But my work would lead me north and that is where I would find my Vietnamese home.

Leaving Home

It was time to again head back to Australia but this time it would only be for a short period as I gave my notice at the Ombudsman's Office and made some preparations to move back to Vietnam in the not too distant future.

For how long that would be and where it would lead me, I didn't really know. At that point in my life, plans and timeframes had no relevance for me and I would go and live each day and see what the next would bring. Any time in my life that I really needed something to happen, it usually did and I thought this would be no different. I knew that if I lived my life in a good manner then good things would come and that philosophy has served me well.

The hardest part of leaving Australia was telling my kids and my mum and trying to explain why. My mum didn't really know a great deal about the world outside as she had never travelled abroad and had only really visited Newcastle and Sydney when she had to; her life was in Gunnedah and that is where she would always stay. She had always been supportive of me and she was once again; although initially not knowing why I should go, she has seen my work evolve over the years and has always backed anything I decide to do. Telling my kids was a tougher assignment and although we all knew to some extent this would happen, the actual parting was never going to be easy. I wasn't just down the highway anymore—I would be overseas, living in a completely different country.

My boys were in their early twenties and already tradesmen living their lives as they chose, so I was reasonably comfortable that they would find their own way as they moved forward. But I also knew from past experience that for them it was still good to have their dad nearby to talk through things that may affect their lives.

Maddy, on the other hand, was still quite young. With her I felt some comfort that she was working and living with family and that her big brothers were close by to support her if needed. She is my baby girl no matter how old she is, so leaving her for a distant country was going to be difficult. Later, we would share some time together in Vietnam that had its share of upsets and happiness, a true adventure that we will never forget.

If I am to be brutally honest, the only regret I had was not spending another four or so years with her so that I could have been there for those times a daughter needs her dad to talk to. Although in Australia we lived some distance apart it would have been nice to play a greater role and to watch as she grew into the wonderful young woman she is today. We were always very close so I knew I was leaving a gap in both of our lives but I also knew that we would both get through that. Right then, at that point in time, in my heart I knew it was time for me to go, otherwise it may have never happened.

Over a period of time I sat with them all and told them my reasons for leaving. I had given them 26 years of my life and during that time I had done all that I thought I could to ensure they would be set up for a good life. Although I valued each moment with them, I just needed to do something selfish, something for me—I wanted to explore and live my life to its fullest. We were living in different cities and although we had some special times together on odd weekends I could not just be around waiting for the time they needed me, or felt they wanted to share. I wanted to spend the rest of my days in a way that would also enhance my life.

I was not the ideal dad but I thought I had done ok, so now it was my time. Although our time together was to be less frequent it would actually have more value because of the limited time that we would have and how we would share that time. It certainly wasn't easy and it would take them time to understand—and I don't mean only a few days, but a year or two. Today, we all share a great relationship and although they would like to see more of me, and I of them, they do understand and share in my life as it is and admire the work I do, and quite possibly the man and dad I am. In Vietnam, I have kids who I support that number into the hundreds but none could ever compare to the four I left behind.

All that was needed to be done was done; now I just waited to board the plane to see what lay ahead.

Sam

Maddy

Jase, Emma, Eli

Matt

Vicki, Maddy

Grandsons Nate and Eli

**Granddaughter Blakely with mum Tash Daphne Heather
with dad Matt**

Vietnam

So it was that once more I would arrive in Hanoi but this time with no expectation of what was to be and no real inclination to know. I would just take each day as it came; my time here might be a few months, years or forever, I didn't know. I just knew that this was where I was meant to be.

Prior to coming to Vietnam I applied for and was successful in gaining a paid position as a trainer of trainers with the Ho Chi Minh Communist Youth Union. The position was sponsored by the Australian Government and I was given a twelve-month contract. The Youth Union is the largest employer in the Vietnamese Government sector and has staff in all cities, towns and villages throughout Vietnam. It has many programs that assist the youth in Vietnam and one of their biggest programs each year is to encourage thousands upon thousands of Vietnamese youth from high schools and universities to volunteer within their communities for a two-week period during the summer. It's a wonderful program that teaches the youth in Vietnam the importance of giving back to their communities and the meaning of compassion. On completing their studies, many university students here will take a gap year, not to travel but to volunteer. They work for a year to help others while they can before they start a career and family because then they may not have the time to help others as they would like.

Of course students are also taught about communism and their country's history, famous people who have come before and how what they have achieved came to be. I will not spend much time talking about communism as I am not learned enough to do so, but in a recent independent survey Vietnam was voted the fifth happiest country in the world. Talk of a lack of freedom of speech and other rights that the West chooses to believe are ignored. When I compare to the West nowadays with all of its 'freedoms', I can't help but feel this is not necessarily a bad thing. Vietnam has many freedoms and each of its people have the right to run their own commercial enterprises, to buy land and houses, and to live a relatively free life. Most criticisms of this country come from outside the country, not within.

For two months I lived in a small flat that was arranged for me in a district called Hoan Kiem. This area is the main tourist area and it was not really somewhere I wanted to stay but in the first instance it would do until I became acclimatised and found something else. I didn't come to Vietnam to live around tourists nor to live in a foreign enclave in an area like Tay Ho, where most foreign expats live in Hanoi. I came to discover everything I could about Vietnam and to live among its people, in the manner they lived, and Hoan Kiem would not provide that for me. All of my life I had lived with Westerners and I didn't come to Vietnam to do that again; it was now time to see how the East lived and I would do that in the most authentic way that I could.

My time with the Youth Union was very interesting and I met some wonderful people who worked there and I was also very happy to see the amount of work they did with the youth in Vietnam. Almost all students who attend university also spend a short period of time with the military, sometimes on weekends or maybe in a block of a couple of weeks. This had something to do with readiness should a war happen, but again was more of an education about history and how many times Vietnam had to fight to retain their own freedom and way of life against foreign invaders. In Vietnam, it is very important to retain the traditions of the past and to acknowledge those who have gone before, whose sacrifices have allowed the youth of today the freedoms they now have. Their system produces some well-educated and caring young people, and also gives them the tools to become future leaders in a variety of fields.

I left Hoan Kiem within two months and rented a house in Hai Ba Trung district near the Red River, a river that has its origins in China, eventually coming to Hanoi and passing through on its way east. Its name originates from the reddish-brown colour of the water due to the silt it carries during the flood season. There were numerous blackouts in our area as Hanoi then struggled to meet the electrical needs of its people (approximately 12 million) and the infrastructure and buildings required to house them all. We always had enough warning of when they would occur via the loudspeaker system that exists throughout Vietnam, even in rural villages. It is used to provide news and weather forecasts, along with communist broadcasts about the party and what they were doing for the people. I didn't mind the blackouts, as a matter of fact I quite enjoyed them.

During blackouts in the summer months it was so hot and humid that it was almost impossible for people to stay in their houses without air conditioning or fans unless there was a breeze blowing through the house, which was rare. So everybody would grab their small plastic chairs and move out to the alleyway where they lived; somebody would always have some tea to drink and others might bring some fruit or snacks to be shared. It was a good time to share with your neighbours, a little like a block party. Everybody just sat and chatted until the power returned and they slowly made their way back inside.

Life was not expensive in Vietnam and as I had a small amount of money saved I knew that I would survive at least for another year before times got a little desperate after leaving the Youth Union. I also knew that something would arrive in some form or another that would inevitably send me down another pathway that was usually for the best.

I did a little work for a man called Son in his volunteer service; it was one of a number in Hanoi but I was not really happy with the way it was run and the others seem to lack a personal touch so it was down this pathway I would go.

First a small verse on how to give help rather than condemn and turn a person into an outcast. Sometimes a little patience and understanding is needed.

A monk had twelve young trainees at his pagoda
in the mountains.
The trainees had issues with one of their own as he was stealing
food and other items from their dormitory.
They requested a meeting with the monk and asked that he do
something about the trainee.
The monk told them to go about their training [and] not to be
concerned as he would change his ways.
This did not occur and again they requested another meeting,
still the same reply from the monk.
They requested a third meeting and at this meeting they told the
monk that if he did not get rid of that particular trainee they
would all leave.
The monk told them, "If that is what you want then leave now,
it is obvious you do not need my help, but he does."
Nothing else was said, the trainees stayed and the one they
wanted removed changed his ways with their help.

Some other work that I really did enjoy was working with university students and formalising their volunteer work. Vietnam has a lot of volunteer activities for students during the summer holidays but I set up groups that would assist others more consistently. The students were all wonderful young people and were very passionate about helping disadvantaged children and people in their communities. I just needed to provide a little structure and together we would source the programs or individuals we thought would benefit most from our help. We did some small fundraisers but primarily just went to various programs weekly and helped where we could. Thuong, a young woman with one of the groups, would later become my first volunteer coordinator in Hanoi until her own vocation called.

This time was a little like the times when as a parent I watched my kids playing sport and thought how differently I would do it if I was the coach. So that time had arrived again. In life you sometimes learn from the achievements of others, sometimes from their failures or shortcomings. Although it had never entered my mind when coming to Vietnam, I knew that I could run a volunteer service and that I could do it in a manner far different to other services, a service that would meet the needs of the beneficiaries before anything else and also a service that would be family oriented and friendly for volunteers. I didn't want to have a service that would bring volunteers halfway around the world and would simply meet their perceived needs, but one that would see volunteers have a truly meaningful impact on the lives of the many disadvantaged children and people here. That would happen and that program would come, but the time was not right yet—a little later.

While waiting to put this in place, I went to Sapa to do some volunteering for a friend I had also met through Tuan. Her name is Shu Tan and she is a Hmong woman. According to the Vietnamese Government there are fifty-three ethnic minority groups in Vietnam (fifty-four including the Vietnamese, who are known as the Kinh or Viet). Kinh Viet comprise eighty-six per cent of the population of Vietnam. As a young woman, Shu Tan was creating pathways for the children of her community to achieve much more in life than selling trinkets on the streets or working the family's small plot of land to survive. She had started a small school and I enjoyed three wonderful months living, volunteering and exploring the wonders of the region.

Sapa is very much a tourist town, attracting almost a million domestic and foreign tourists each year. It is famous for its magnificent mountain scenery, terraced rice paddies, streams and waterfalls, and it also has the distinction of being home to Mount Fansipan—standing at 3,143 metres, it is the highest mountain in South East Asia.

Among all of this beauty there is also much poverty within the ethnic tribes. All of the businesses in Sapa at that time were owned by Kinh Viet or were foreign invested. The ethnic minority people were and are exploited by these businesses as they are the real attraction to Sapa and the only gain they get out of this massive tourist trade is selling goods on the streets, being underpaid in restaurants and hotels, selling trinkets as children or acting as guides. For me, the ultimate indignity was to see travel organisations using their own Kinh Viet people as guides. Ethnic minority children would complete primary school, as it was compulsory, and then go and sell trinkets on the streets or help the family survive by producing agriculture on very small mountainous plots of land.

Shu Tan was the first ethnic minority person in her region to complete high school and she then set up a classroom to help educate kids in English language to help them to sell better to tourists. As they had their own dialect, she also taught them Vietnamese to help them find better employment or vocational training opportunities. She opened the first ethnic minority business in Sapa, a small café and guide business, and has continued to make other strides forward.

I really enjoyed life in Sapa as it didn't take long to know the locals and being a friend of Shu Tan's I knew virtually everyone in town. Only one thing unsettled me more than anything else; the rampant and open domestic violence in the area and the beatings that some of the kids and women took. Most men in the communities drank rice wine and it didn't really matter what time of day it took place. This is another education process that needs to take place, with a real need for people in the communities to take control of that process. I don't think I will see the day that men consume less but to think of a world without it would be nice. Alcohol has so many bad side effects on society in general.

I loved my teaching work with the kids and setting up games and activities. On some days most of the children were available but on other days they had to work to help their families make ends meet. They were a wonderful bunch of kids and had a strong woman as their leader and role model. It was a pleasure to know them and also to call Shu Tan a friend. I left as winter arrived and the mist became so thick that you could barely see twenty feet in front of you. Sapa is the only place in Vietnam you will find snow but that could be five to ten years' apart, and only for a couple of days at most.

I returned to the house in Hai Ba Trung and enlisted another friend to build a website for me which, again, was to bring change. This change would really define me, at times bring me to tears and at other times provide overwhelming joy. The volunteer service we created was called the Vietnam International Volunteer Placement Service (VIVPS)—I guess that said it all, but some six years later I changed the name to the Red Lotus Foundation (RLF) and that is how it will be referred to throughout the book. I decided on the change because I didn't think the name VIVPS accurately represented me anymore, nor the nature of the work we do.

The lotus flower is a national symbol of Vietnam and the red lotus represents love and compassion. I added the word 'foundation' not because we were like a foundation/charity but because love and compassion are the foundation/roots from which we grow and are what we represent.

In terms of volunteer arrivals they dropped off slightly while people adapted to the change of name and we grew our Google ranking again, but numbers and money were never important. I have always only needed enough to pay my staff and for me to live a very simple life, as our priority has and always will be the children who we serve. How we could best serve them would take time to evolve and came through another program I implemented, called Helping Hands Vietnam (HHV). Everybody associated with both services is guided by those four basic tenets: love, compassion, understanding and truth. If people do not carry those principles, they don't work for us; if volunteers cannot abide by them, they are in the wrong place. COVID changed the world in many different ways and when it was over I decided to shut the volunteer service down, I now had a baby daughter to care for and to be absolutely honest, I was tired and it just felt that the time was right. We still have past volunteers/friends coming for visits to the centre and we help arrange everything for them but do not provide the service we did, they now know the kids and the centre well enough.

Everything has an ending but for now this is how it began.

After the website was designed it was not difficult to find programs to help, as I had travelled and volunteered at quite a few centres and I knew they would appreciate our help. I went back to Saigon for three months and volunteered with Chi Cu again at Truong Tinh orphanage and at the same time set up other programs in Hanoi.

Our relationship with Chi Cu lasted for another three years before she was told by the government that she could not have foreign volunteers at the centre due to the fact she had to go through a complicated registration process, something she had not yet begun. This was going to take some time and, as I was confident that she now had the support in place to assist her in running her program, we did not return there again with RLF, I just visited whenever I was in Saigon.

I didn't feel it necessary to place volunteers at any centre where there was not a real need. I now had Thuong who was coordinating volunteer activities at a couple of programs in Hanoi, and in Saigon I had another Thuong and later Thu, who would assist volunteers until the orphanage program finished.

I also spent some time living in Dalat, a place where we did not set up programs, as this was more of a 'me' thing again. I had visited Dalat for a few days some time before and thought how wonderful it would be to live there for a short time. The few centres that were in Dalat were quite well resourced so I didn't see the need to advertise for volunteers to come there. I did, however, have two volunteers request to work in Dalat and our very first volunteer, Christina from Canada, was one of them. I also had volunteers who, after completing their time with Chi Cu in Saigon, would come to Dalat to meet up and I would be their tour guide and show them the beautiful country that surrounds the town and also introduce them to the way of life there. During my time there I volunteered at three centres—not on a daily basis but I went to each when time permitted and helped out wherever they felt I could be best utilised.

Dalat is in the central highlands and is known as the city of flowers, or the city of eternal love. The names aptly describe the city as they grow flowers and export them all over the world, and each year many newlyweds go there to honeymoon. It has a beautiful climate all year round, it is never too hot or too cold; a lovely town surrounded by mountains and pine forests. Dalat has many wonderful coffee shops but I used to spend most mornings at a little out-of-the-way coffee shop that was very simple in set up and not so well known. The shop was run by a lovely woman and her husband and it afforded a very peaceful ambience and a magnificent view across a valley to distant mountains. I would usually go there alone just to relax and enjoy the view and always left refreshed and with an overwhelming feeling of peace, as the café was very meditative. As I write about the town now I get the same feeling as before; it's amazing how much I miss that place and the peace it can still bring to me simply by thought.

I returned to Hanoi, where I was to live permanently and become more invested in the day-to-day operations of RLF, and where I would again find opportunities to volunteer and help out when I could. This is also the time when I met the most influential person in my life to date—my best friend, my confidant, one of my teachers and most importantly, one with whom I would share a mutual love and respect and together share both the sadness and joys of life. No, I am not speaking of my future wife as this relationship was never like that; it was just a friendship, but a very special one, one that endured and still does today in spirit, for now we are many kilometres apart. Her name is Hanh and she replaced Thuong as the RLF coordinator in Hanoi.

Hanh

I have found that so many young people of the Buddhist faith in Vietnam have a view of life that gives them not only peace, but also a way of understanding the complexities of life as they are confronted with them. There were many occasions during our time together that Hanh taught me how to simplify my life and to focus on the things that were important to me, and not those that I could not control: To also leave my Western viewpoints behind and to think more like a Vietnamese person living in this time and space. I had stepped back in time and it didn't need Vietnam to adjust to suit me, I was the one who needed to understand and adjust.

I had always adopted the mindset that life should be taken one step at a time and to not concern myself with the larger world but to focus on mine, and Hanh reinforced that when needed. None of us are perfect and we often stray, so when that happens it is best to find your way back as quickly as possible and if you happen to have guidance from somebody who can speak with reason, clarity and simplicity, then all the better.

When I strayed, I needed a Hanh as she was that someone who kept me grounded and focused with the simplest of words or sayings. Hanh did that for me and I for her when she had a need and if I had wisdom enough to counsel her. There was a time when I was feeling a little lost and not sure what my next step would be and Hanh sensed this so we talked briefly about my feelings. Her response was immediate and very incisive—she simply said, "You are where you are meant to be, aren't you?" That was not the first time I had heard this but such was her ability to say so very little and yet be so insightful. With another, it may have been a counselling session for the next hour with endless talk about the things bothering me and why did I feel this way? None of that was necessary, all that needed to be said had been said with those ten little words.

Don't question it, just live it
If you don't like it, then change it
Zet

We had a unique relationship, one that we both cherished, and she was to stay with me as the RLF coordinator for approximately four years; she was loved not only by me but by many volunteers, friends and family from all over the world. Together we discovered a program that would change us both very dramatically and give us both a different view of the work we shared and the direction it should take. We were assisted by other wonderful people like Kim Anh, Ngan, Hang Luu, Hang and Luan in this important initial phase of our RLF working lives.

Hang, Volunteer Jen, Luan,
Ngan

Thuong, Thuong, Hanh

Hang Luu

Kim Anh

Thu

Been

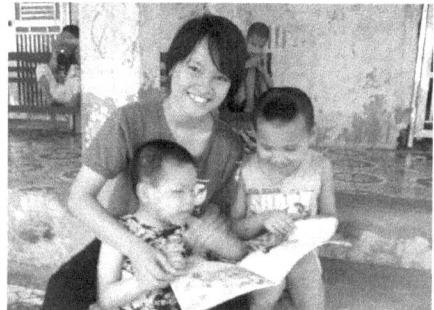

Muoi

Hanh was a city girl and I a foreigner, both of us with a thirst to discover the rural areas outside of Hanoi and to find and spend time in villages that were not even on maps. So, when not working, we would take my motorbike and just head out of Hanoi on a road we had not previously taken and see what lay ahead. We discovered many beautiful country locations and ancient pagodas to visit and enjoyed the hospitality of many people in small villages scattered around the north. The roads that we didn't get to take I would later ride with my soon-to-be wife, Thuy. Hanh is now married to one of our ex-volunteers, Sven and is living very happily in Austria with two beautiful young children.

Volunteers

The service was running very well as we had a good flow of volunteers for the few programs that we had, and we firmly believed in the service that we were providing. Once a volunteer entered Vietnam they became our responsibility, as we needed to register them with the local authorities so that they could work at a centre. We were accountable for all of their actions during their time with us, both at the centre and outside it; we have been very lucky that our volunteers behaved well while in this country and we had no major incidents that would require police action. But providing a service is not always smooth sailing. We have had three volunteers hospitalised for extended periods of time and have provided support to many others in many different ways.

One young woman came to us from the USA and unbeknown to her had the onset of meningitis, a very dangerous disease that can kill within hours. She became very ill and not knowing what was wrong, we had her hospitalised; when she was diagnosed with the disease we then had to arrange for her parents to get here as quickly as they could to get her safely home for further treatment. Another was a young woman who did not disclose to us that she had abdominal epilepsy, a disease normally found in children, so she too was hospitalised for a few days and rested up in my house for a few more after that.

Our other unfortunate case was a man from New Zealand aged fifty-seven who collapsed and suffered a seizure while on a field trip with a group of kids from a centre. He was diagnosed with epilepsy and considering it was the first time this had occurred in his life, it was a great shock. He needed time to come to grips with what happened and it took some time before he felt safe to fly, so we again monitored and supported him. Of course we have taken many a volunteer to doctors and clinics with minor illnesses and some cuts and bruises but that is just part of our daily lives, although things do seem to be magnified when you are so far from home.

I had one volunteer who made disclosures to me about sexual abuse that had occurred in her childhood; we spent a lot of time together so that she could release a little of the pain and together we developed a management plan for when she returned home to confront the abuser and accomplices.

We have had our fair share of people with depression, some who have notified us in advance and have said that they were fine with medication and others who did not tell us. One particular person who did not disclose spent almost an entire week threatening to commit suicide. He had been with us for a couple of weeks and exhibited some strange behaviours and had also confided in us some of the troubles he had experienced in his life, but it still came as a shock to us all when he threatened to commit suicide. We counselled and monitored him as best we could and encouraged him to return home as early as possible to deal with his issues, which he ended up doing.

I have had many volunteers stay at my house for a variety of reasons and have been happy to have them. I would make myself available to listen and, if I felt I could provide some advice, I would do so as best I could. It is amazing what people carry with them to volunteer and also how many believe that volunteering to help others will help them. That may well be the case in some circumstances but certainly not for most. My house is open to staff and volunteers and they are all welcome to come and stay in the good times and the not so good.

One of the hardest situations my staff and I found ourselves in was trying to help someone suffering from culture shock. I remember when I first set foot in Saigon and what a shock it was to me—the weather, the traffic, the language, the food and, for me, no foreigners to be seen. I would soon overcome that and any shock replaced with excitement and new experiences, but for others culture shock and the fear that comes with that are very real. Most first-time travellers come and, like me, after a short time they adjust, but not all can. The first of these was a young man from America.

He arrived in the afternoon and that evening went out with some other volunteers who were here at the time; everything seemed fine with him, he appeared happy and was enjoying himself but the next morning he woke in a very confused and nervous state and immediately wanted to go home and wouldn't provide an explanation. It is possible that something happened at home but that seemed unlikely as he was just very fearful and teary. I said we would take him to a travel agent and he could change his ticket but he would not have any of that, he insisted on going to the airport to change his ticket and waiting there. So we took him to the airport and when he had his ticket and was possibly more comfortable and familiar with all of the foreigners coming and going, a change occurred and he apologised. He said he could not explain why but he just had to go, and in a few hours' time he did just that.

The next was a young woman from New York who also arrived early afternoon, but did not even arrive at the guesthouse before ringing her family and telling them that she wanted to return home. Nothing untoward happened from the airport to the house, just what I had witnessed some years before—lots of vehicles, motorbikes, honking horns and an endless stream of people, but it was too much for her. We tried to appease her during the afternoon and she was in the company of a number of volunteers who had been with us for weeks but nothing they or I could say would change the way she felt. Later that evening I took her to a travel agent and she changed her flight to the next day and I could see her immediately relax when she knew that had been done. But right at the end of the process the agent said, "The ticket is booked and we just need to confirm it in the morning as it is too late to do it now." With those words, she immediately burst into tears and although the travel agent and I knew the ticket would be ok, she would not have it. I ended up asking her what time it was in New York and suggesting that she ring her parents to book a flight there and have it confirmed. They did that and again she relaxed; she stayed the night and left the next day but would not eat anything but boiled rice and drink nothing but bottled water.

Our other situation was a mature woman from Alaska who had been with us at the centre for two days. One afternoon we came back to find her at the guesthouse in tears with a couple of other volunteers talking to her. She knew exactly what was wrong with her and told us she first felt it when she arrived in Hanoi and went to the hotel. She was to stay in Hanoi for the weekend and join the program on the Monday but what we didn't know is that while in Hanoi she did not leave the hotel at any stage except for her orientation with us. She never disclosed it at the time but said that she felt a fear of the crowds and the noise so she had her meals in the room and didn't leave the hotel until she came out to us. She had worked in remote communities in Alaska and the difference between her and the other two people was that she knew what was happening and tried to work through it, though unfortunately, by herself. She could not progress and was determined to leave so we just had to help her make the arrangements. She is a wonderful lady and when she returned home she did a fundraiser for our HHV program and still keeps tabs on us.

It was such a useless feeling trying to help the three of them as there is so little anyone can do, we just had to support them as best we could and try to be understanding of their situation. It was really difficult as I had never experienced anything like it and if I had to try to explain it in layman's terms, to me it seemed as though they were having a prolonged anxiety attack and the only cure was a plane ticket. I guess in the end they learned a lot more about themselves and the frailties we all have in one form or another.

We provide a service and are very happy to do so in pleasant circumstances and in some difficult circumstances, like those above. I have a responsibility to all of our volunteers, as do my staff and we try to provide the best we can to all. There are our wonderful volunteers who return to us year after year, those that fundraise for HHV, and those that may only be able to make one trip but still remain friends for life and help us in their own little way when needed. We have a huge family with whom we share love, and that family stretches across every continent.

Thuy An Caring Centre

We were working with a couple of programs in Hanoi and our volunteers were certainly happy, but I didn't feel that I was doing enough. I wasn't fully satisfied that my contribution through RLF was achieving or making a difference to the disadvantaged peoples of Vietnam the way that I hoped it would. One day, Hanh told me of a friend who knew of a centre located in Thuy An Village, Ba Vi province, a centre that she felt was in need of volunteers but as far as she knew had never had any. We arranged to go to Ba Vi the following week to visit and assess the centre and in doing that my life would change again—a stern test of my character but also the most rewarding thing I have done with my life; my four tenets were about to be truly tested.

The village is approximately sixty-five kilometres from Hanoi so again we boarded the bike and rode out into the country. Ba Vi is a beautiful rural area and is more of an attraction for Vietnamese tourists who usually come from Hanoi than it is for foreigners. It has Ba Vi Mountain, which affords a wonderful view of the surrounding area, rice fields, pineapple crops, small lakes and other assorted agriculture, and the area also has some beautiful pagodas. That was not why we were here but later as the program progressed, Ba Vi province would provide some great cross-cultural moments for our volunteers and give them a true insight into what life was like for people in rural Vietnam. As we were the only foreigners in the area, the locals soon got to know us well and many international friendships would be established between our volunteers and the local villagers.

The centre itself was hard to take in and the conditions that the kids lived in were quite distressing, to say the least. Although I had

148

travelled extensively from the north to the south volunteering at many centres, and I had also seen the effects that Agent Orange had on generations of families in central Vietnam, I had never seen a centre such as this; it was completely under-resourced.

This centre would effect me and many others that would come a little later in a manner so difficult to describe. These little human beings and the centre itself needed help and it was as if Duyen (fate) had stepped in and given us the opportunity to do just that.

Vietnam at the time was rated a third-world country but this went way beyond that, and on that day I could only wonder why?

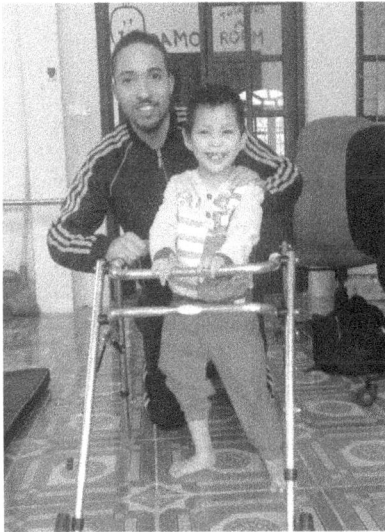

Grown Men Do Cry

The kids were confined to the inside of the rooms and if they couldn't walk, they never saw the outside of the room. If they couldn't crawl then a steel cot with no mattress was home 24/7 as they would sweat so much during the summer and with a mattress this in itself would have health issues, only during the short cooler months was a mattress provided. Those that could crawl would be lifted out of their cots, placed on the cement floor and allowed to crawl to some chairs. This, to the staff, was part of their rehabilitation—to let them crawl and give them help with a gentle touch of the foot and I believe to some degree they were right as it was the only form of physical activity the kids had.

Each room contained steel cots that would sleep up to six children. The rooms stank of faeces and urine as the children were only changed three times a day; what that meant was if they had a change and say, thirty minutes later, soiled their nappy they would remain in that state until it was time for all to be changed again, maybe four or five hours later. The children didn't actually have nappies as we would think of them—they were wrapped in old clothing, shirts, pants or whatever type of rags could be found. Rooms at the top end of the centre had old steel doors and they were locked except when the staff needed to access the children.

There was one room that appeared to be over-resourced in comparison to the others—Room 8, the nursery. This was a room for babies and toddlers most without disabilities who were either abandoned or given up for adoption. The room had everything the others did not but should have—big thick mattresses on all beds, an over-abundance of staff, air conditioning, television, clean clothing, disposable nappies—and they were cared for in a way that all the children at the centre should have been. I certainly didn't begrudge these toddlers anything at all and was very happy to see the way that they were cared for; I only wished it was the same for all. This was the one room any foreigners would come to if they came to the centre as they usually came for adoptions and so it was given far superior resources and kept very clean and hygienic.

When we started bringing volunteers to the centre we would try as best we could to make them comfortable and some who really struggled at the centre would often end up spending their time in the nursery. One day I went to the nursery and we had five volunteers in the room playing with or nursing babies, and only two in the other rooms trying to work with the kids with disabilities. On that day, approximately two years into our time at the centre I made a decision that volunteers would be informed before arriving that they could not work in the nursery as it was well resourced and we felt that the need in other rooms was far greater.

Volunteers were allowed to go to the nursery and spend time with the toddlers at the end of our work day but if you came to RLF you came knowing full well that you would be working with children with disabilities. I am very understanding of our volunteers' desire to visit and spend time in the nursery and am happy to make that time available, but if we really wanted to make a difference here it would not be in the well-resourced nursery but in the other rooms.

I am no expert on disabilities—I bring experts to help guide our work here and although over ten years my knowledge has grown, I didn't need to be an expert this first day, for I was sure that if I was given an extensive list of both intellectual and physical disabilities they would all be found here. There are approximately 180 children in the centre at any given time and an equal number of adults who live in an area I named The Block. The Block is a name given to a block of housing in Redfern, Sydney; houses on The Block were purchased over several decades by the Aboriginal Housing Company (AHC) and the area is viewed by the largely rural Aboriginal population of New South Wales as a spiritual home in Australia's largest city. Although this area is completely different in nature, I do get a spiritual feeling similar to the one I get when I visit the Redfern Block.

After that first day, on our way to meet with the directors, I tried to take in what I had just seen and how, in such a short time, it had affected me in such a way that I felt overwhelmed. I knew one thing for certain and that was that I could not walk away and abandon these kids. I was confident that over time I would find a way to make their life a little more bearable. It wasn't the time to strategise and think too far ahead as we still didn't know if we would have permission to do anything here.

Our meeting with the directors went well and if our registration was approved by the local authority, we would be allowed to work here. I didn't say a great deal beyond stating who I was and how I thought that if we worked together we could enhance the wellbeing of the kids under their care. No volunteer group had ever been allowed to work at the centre and none has since we arrived. I am not sure why we were given permission but I was grateful for the opportunity to help as best I could. I wanted a program where we could make a difference, not just somewhere to place volunteers, and here it was. We hopped on the bike again and headed back to Hanoi, this time with a tear or two in our eyes. Ahead of me was a short time to reflect and then the hardest but also the most emotionally rewarding challenge of my life.

From that first day through to today, each time I walk through the gates at the centre I have to remind myself that, in terms of service for these wonderful young kids, I am going back some 30 to 40 years from my current Western views. This is what it was like back then and I can remember some of the history of caring centres in my country in those times. So I can go back reasonably easily but when we have a young volunteer who was only born 20-something years ago, it is hard for me to educate them so they can make a comparison. It is very emotional and there are no bad people here, just people living in a different time and space to us.

It took a little time after advertising the program for any volunteers to apply but soon we had a steady flow and although we had good relationships with our other programs in Hanoi I was confident enough to know they would survive without our help as they already had good support systems in place. Ba Vi would be very time consuming, not only because of the work involved with our volunteers but because of our desire to be there personally.

So it was that we chose to have only one program to advertise and if volunteers were to come to work with RLF, it would be in Ba Vi. I would still take a day or two occasionally to volunteer at some smaller centres where we did not place volunteers. One of those was the Quyen Hoa Centre that is operated by a lovely caring couple. The centre has some very severely disabled residents and I used to go there once a week with either Kim Anh or Hanh to teach some English. The majority of these young people were great learners and very enthusiastic, and it was a joy to meet with them on a regular basis. Over the years some would leave the centre for independent living and we still remain very close friends.

We (and I will use that word a lot instead of 'I' for although I had ultimate responsibility I was never alone and would do almost everything with input from my staff and family of friends) now needed to make some tough decisions at the centre as to where to prioritise our work and that of our volunteers. We are only a small service so we could not possibly cover the 180 kids that were here and we really couldn't let volunteers wander off on their own without our support and oversight. The staff at the centre were not all that welcoming at this time, as we interfered with their schedules and also now with so many eyes on them some practices would need to stop or be quickly reported. At that time, the kids were housed in seven rooms; now there are eight, a result of a program being shut down in Hanoi and twenty-seven kids being transferred to Ba Vi just over six years ago.

Rooms 1 and 2 contained the youngest of the children with disabilities while Rooms 3 and 4 contained much older kids with more severe disabilities, many with cerebral palsy and varying degrees of paralysis. When you looked at their frail bodies you would think they were a young child, but in these two rooms a lot of the kids were in fact late teens or into their mid and late twenties. Rooms 5 and 6 contained older children, most again with physical disabilities but more with intellectual disabilities. The longer a child was at the centre, the clearer one could see a gradual decline in their wellbeing and general health; it was a very sad sight and the staff had very little help in improving their health. Better resources and training were very much needed.

Here, I should really point out that although I tend to paint a poor picture of the centre staff, it should also be noted that they have never had any consistent training in dealing with children with disabilities and were only set minimal tasks each day by the powers that be, who also have little training. They are just local country people who are lucky enough to be working; the majority have no professional expertise whatsoever and the centre has only one senior nurse and a very small nursing unit. Unfortunately there appeared to be little oversight and for children with such severe disabilities little resources given. There are so many children in Vietnam in the same situation we find our children here in Ba Vi that it is a huge task for the government to find the necessary resources and training to give to all, but time changes all; they are trying. There is more training now, better funding, and we need to be patient for as this country grows, so too will the operations of centres such as these.

We decided that the best thing we could do was to focus on the younger children and try to make change before they too started to go backwards. So we commenced work with our volunteers in Rooms 1 and 2 and, if numbers allowed, we would also work with the kids in Rooms 3 and 4, and then move to Rooms 5 and 6. Over the years, our returning volunteers would just go to the rooms and the kids they were familiar with, as everyone had their favourite rooms, with some choosing the younger kids and others choosing the older ones. Although saddened by their conditions the volunteers did not want to see them miss out on the little joys that life and interaction with others can provide— the little things that I encouraged, like a smile a day.

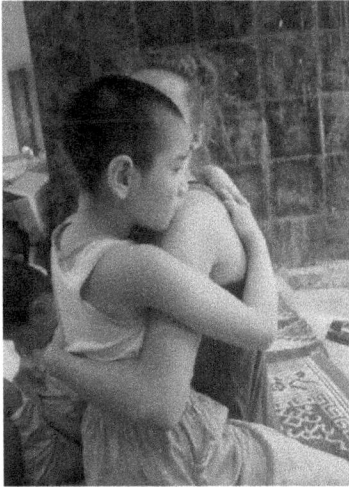

Special Moments

We needed to get the kids outside in the fresh air and provide them with some activities that would stimulate their minds, strengthen their core muscles and, equally as important, we needed to have them smile and laugh and feel loved, something that was at times foreign to them here. This would create a number of issues, as previously there were no activities and there was no 'outside'. Vietnam is a very hot country but in the north of Vietnam there is a winter and although short it can become quite chilly. So when we asked the staff to take the kids outside, most of the time we would be told, "It's too hot and sunny"; "It's too cold" or "It's too wet".

This was a frustrating time as we were aware of the weather and would not take the kids out in extreme conditions, but they did need to experience the different elements and they certainly needed a little sunshine—a plant can't grow without the sun and at that time we were growing mushrooms but we wanted flowers. They needed vitamin D and also the brain stimulation that comes with sunshine, a definite mood enhancer. The sunshine vitamin is also good for your muscles and in limited amounts it is good for both physical and mental wellbeing.

When we had the opportunity to get the kids outside, we would grab a few grass mats, toys, puzzles, books and whatever other form of stimulation we had bought, and this was a very special time for the children. It was a very simplistic start to the program but I knew it was not enough; this is when HHV had its beginning. It would not start with a bang and had no need to—like everything else I do, it was one step at a time. We started with a small fundraiser in Hanoi and we purchased a good quantity of nappies and milk for the kids, but there were more pressing issues that needed to be addressed before I could really claim any advances here. I would next address the issue of getting the kids outside on a more regular basis and how best to address rehabilitation.

Humble beginnings

Rooms 1, 2, 3 and 4 did have large, fenced areas out the front of the rooms but they were very open, with no shelter; hence the hesitation from staff when we tried to get the kids outside. I have learned throughout life that, if confronted with some form of roadblock, you find a way around it, knock it down or, if it is beyond destruction, find an alternate route. I needed to address the outside access and weather issues, so through HHV we built some very big shelters that would provide shade from the sun and shelter from the rains; to combat the heat we bought some very big commercial-type fans. We also had people in the local village build us some tables and benches that the kids could sit around and use for activities. Around this time we also started to purchase some wheelchairs and special support chairs for our most severe cases so that we could have virtually all kids come outside in shifts.

Building shelters and purchasing special support chairs and wheelchairs

One thing I was acutely aware of was our responsibility to community development and I enjoy the fact that, when possible, we always use local people for supplies, building items for rooms, food and other purchases that we make. Thuy An and its adjoining villages are very poor so I am happy that we can consistently pay back and help to boost the economy of the area. As I write today, we employ six local people at the centre as well as six residents to help us with our work, so along with the general improvement in the wellbeing of the children, it is also gratifying to know that we contribute to the economic and social development of the local community.

Rooms 5, 6, 7 and the nursery were a little different to address as they had no immediate fenced outdoor area. The rooms opened up into a big quadrangle and we could not just put up a shelter as we did for the other four rooms. We would have to raise the level of the floor to reach the room floor height and on top of that, build an enclosed outdoor area with roofing. We were happy to do that as it would get kids out of that smelly room, where they could breathe some fresh air and feel a little sunshine. As there were some difficult kids in the rooms who would run if given the opportunity, it would keep them safe and yet still provide easy access to the large quadrangle area for the kids who could be trusted to not run away. So we built another four shelters and suddenly we had given access to all children at the centre to a limited, but nonetheless outside world.

The next thing I knew we needed to do was address the lack of rehabilitation. We had advertised for specialist help on our website and they were arriving in the form of physical therapists, occupational therapists, one acupuncture specialist, teachers and nurses who would have to practise their occupations on the floor outside the rooms or within the crowded rooms—this would not do. It also was at this time that I would meet a young woman who would be instrumental in the building of all things medical we did for our HHV team.

Her name is Katie and we met in Hanoi when a service for which she had volunteered gave her a far from satisfactory experience. Katie was working at a program in Hanoi that was shut down because it was found that the director of that private orphanage centre was selling babies off to China. That is how we came to have those children transferred to the centre and how they would occupy what became Room 7. We met in Hanoi and Katie who is a paediatric nurse from England asked if she could come out to the centre for a few days to catch up with the children from the other centre to see if they were alright. I told her I would be very happy to have her out there and she could stay as long as she liked but little did I know that she would take me up on that offer literally. I have been married to my wife Thuy for eight years and although I am not too sure how long Katie was with us prior to our wedding, I do know that she was a bridesmaid. A wonderful, caring and compassionate young woman with a love for the kids that has no boundaries, and a work ethic that is beyond what could be expected of anyone. That last sentence also applies to two other young women, Carly and Justine, who I will talk of shortly; I love all three as my own and am humbled to be able to play a small part in their lives.

We raised the funds to build a physiotherapy room and equip it with the necessary items to carry out that work and over time Katie and Justine set up a schedule of kids. In the initial stage, I employed three women to work in that room; during the first two years it was Hang Luu, Chuyen and Tham. Hang Luu also served as the local coordinator and Tham now works in Rooms 3 and 4 as an activity coordinator. Chuyen has been with us since day one of the physio room and now works in partnership with Nang. Neither of these women had any physio experience prior to coming to us and were taught the basics to what their capacities allowed by our visiting physios and physio students. We were always aware of their limitations but the longer they have been with us, the more confident they have become and the more complex the work they are able to do. Our visiting specialists have been wonderful in training our team with much patience and giving freely of their knowledge. Katie also learned from them when time allowed and oversaw the running of the room with assistance from Justine and Carly.

Early days: physio outside on the grass mats and then in the new room

161

Carly from the USA was with us from the very beginning as she was one of our very first volunteers in Ba Vi. She came and went but it was not long before she returned again, and again and again. Carly returns home each year for a few months, then spends the majority of her time here with us and her Vietnam family. I couldn't employ Carly through our HHV program as I had decided that I had an obligation to employ only Vietnamese people in that capacity, with the exception of Katie who plays a leading role in the professional training of our HHV staff. Carly has been and is a vital cog in everything that happens here and is also a de facto RLF marketing person. She is the type who will help anybody in any way that she possibly can. We have worked together at the centre; we have bought cows, repaired roofs, purchased motors for wells, sponsored school fees for children, arranged hospital visits, fundraised for treatment for people with life-threatening illnesses, helped others in the community and enjoyed each other's company through the good and the not so good—another very special human being.

Over the first few years in Ba Vi, with the closure of other programs and a number of other contributing factors, we experienced many staff changes. Four of my previous coordinators have married and now live overseas, while others still here in Vietnam have had babies, limiting their availability, while others have pursued further study or careers not quite so demanding.

You cannot just bring a volunteer to a foreign country, meet and greet, show them the centre and then leave them to their own devices. They also need to be cared for and if they have illnesses or other issues, our Ba Vi coordinator needs to be nearby and ready to take whatever steps are needed to ensure the wellbeing of the volunteer. They also need assistance in acclimatising to a new way of life and different culture. All of our past employees would be welcome back at any time and although they are all a little different, each had the two underlying traits that define a RLF employee: love and compassion. I am very happy to have met and worked with all of them and am honoured to call them my friends. I mentioned another name before, Justine, but before she arrives it is time for me to get married.

Thuy

I met my future wife, Thuy, in a coffee shop in Hanoi. Hanoi has thousands of coffee shops and although I prefer to drink green tea on the streets I have also visited a large number of these coffee shops. I came across a shop not too far from where I lived at the time and as I hadn't been there before I dropped in for a refreshing juice on a very hot day to see what the shop was like. A young woman came to take my order and then gave me my drink but didn't really pay any attention to me at all, possibly because the staff and others seemed quite engrossed in an Indian soap opera that was on the TV at the time, and maybe she wanted to get back to that, or she just didn't fancy me in any way at all.

I fancied her though, so I returned again and this time spoke to her a little in my limited Vietnamese. I liked her look; I thought she had a very kind face, but I was not really fully taken until I saw her run. Funny how love finds us and sometimes it's those quirky little things that draw you to another. It was a small distance from the front of the shop to the back where the cash register was and occasionally when she had to give change she would run back, I guess to hurry along to watch the soap opera again, but as she did so she resembled a little duck waddling along. I found it very cute and along with all of her other wonderful virtues it is the one that still makes me smile today, as she duck-waddles from place to place.

The coffee shop was her sister and brother-in-law's shop and they lived with their four children in the house above the shop. Thuy, I would find out, had a rented room not far from the shop and apart from her work here she had previously worked at a money exchange shop but left because she used to get very scared carrying huge amounts of money each day to the bank, so until we met and both of our lives changed, the coffee shop would be her vocation. During my second visit I asked her if I wanted to see her again outside of the shop, how would I do this? She told me that I would need to come to the shop as she worked from 6 am to around 9 pm every day.

Thuy is from a very small and very poor village in the province of Phu Tho and during her infancy she grew up in her grandmother's very small house with a dusty concrete floor. There was grandma, mum and dad, Thuy and her three brothers and sister, and another uncle, in a one-bedroom house. I would later tile the floors of the house for Ba (Grandma), something she was very grateful for and I was very happy to see her joy when the work was completed. Thuy had only been to one other place when I first met her, and that was Hanoi. A little time before we met she had arranged with a girlfriend from her hometown to visit Nha Trang, a coastal tourist city where her friend now lived and for Thuy, this would be a great adventure for the little lady who had never been anywhere. While she was there we talked every night on Messenger, and basically got to know each other that way.

When she returned we saw a lot more of each other and we knew that this relationship was going somewhere. We were both adults and we wanted to be together more intimately but Thuy was terrified her family would find out, so most nights I would wait for her on my bike about two blocks from the café and we would go to my place. In the morning, I would again drop her off well away from the shop and she would walk to work as if coming from her room. We were like little school kids, sneaking around the corner for a kiss, and we actually quite enjoyed this little drama that we planned each night. My little duck was a lot like me, a little crazy and that enjoyment of life still keeps us as much in love today as we were then. It's ok to be a little crazy as it brings some levity into your life; life wasn't meant to be so serious and our primary focus should be on love and laughter which in turn equal happiness.

It only took about three months before I asked her to marry me and she agreed, but first I had to face the family and get their blessing. Her father still carries shrapnel in his head as a result of the American War and lives in a hospice outside Hanoi, so it was the oldest brother I would have to ask. We arranged to eat at his house one night and with Thuy's mother also present, I pleaded my case and asked for permission. His reply was *'suy nghi da'* which, translated from Vietnamese means, 'I will think about it and tell you later'.

It wasn't exactly the answer I had hoped for but it wasn't a 'no', so I found some solace in that. For the next week, I asked Thuy every day if he had made up his mind yet and the same answer each day was *'chua'*, translation: 'not yet'. He is a police officer, as many of Thuy's extended family are, and he was afraid that if I happened to do something wrong, as a foreigner, it would come back on the family and would hinder his career. After one week, I guess he thought I was of a reasonable character as he gave his blessing.

I thought around six months later would be a good time to get married, as it would give us more time to know each other a little better and to prepare for our life ahead. But here in Vietnam the foreteller decides on the most prosperous time for your wedding to take place, a time when all of the omens align. So it was that Thuy and her mum would head off to the foreteller and on their return told me that we were to be married in three months' time, not six. I was a little apprehensive as everything was moving so quickly but I had no need for apprehension; Thuy is a wonderful wife, a good person and my best mate. I will do all I can to make her life one of only happiness and I know she will do the same for me. We had our marriage celebration at 8.30 am on Wednesday 12th November 2014.

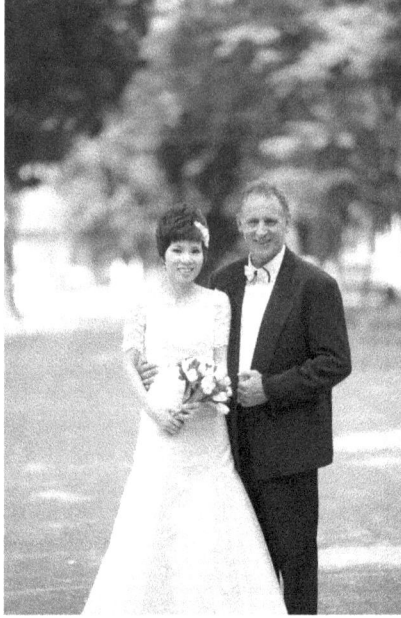

We would have a traditional wedding party in Thuy's hometown but first we had to get our official wedding certificate through the government. Approximately one month prior to the wedding we had our wedding photos taken with me in my tux and Thuy in her bridal and other traditional dresses. The photos were then displayed at the wedding celebration. So, after receiving our certificate from the government, we were officially married. All that remained now was the celebration and the family blessing, which was the most important thing.

Normally the groom would go to the bride's house with his family, meet with her family and then take his bride back to his house for the final celebration. As I had no house or family in Phu Tho, I simply arrived at Thuy's house with my wedding party which consisted of my son Matt who had made the trip over, Katie and four volunteers who were in Ba Vi at that time and who to this day remain lifelong friends: Dorothy, Alicia, Leila and Sarah. We also had the two current RLF coordinators, Luan and Hang Luu, at the wedding, along with Chuyen and Phong.

The day before the ceremony was spent in food preparation and erecting the marquee and to my surprise that night was set aside for family and close friends to party. We had singers and very loud music, as is common here and we danced the night away. It was a great night and a time to relax as the next day would be quite formal. I arrived at Thuy's house a little late the next morning as our bus driver had a little too much to drink the night before and overslept. My little bride looked beautiful as did the women and my Western friends in their Vietnamese traditional Ao Dai dresses. There was a big crowd gathered on the road as we arrived, as I was the first foreigner to marry someone in the village, and everybody was very interested to see it. We entered the house with Thuy, Matt and I to sit at a table opposite Thuy's family. Matt had the task of officially welcoming Thuy to our family and then her father welcomed me to their family. Thuy and I then put some items on the family altar to acknowledge our ancestors and to get their blessing. It was a short ceremony but very significant and we were both a little overcome.

Then we all went to the marquee, welcomed our guests and enjoyed a meal together. This part of the ceremony does not last a long time and there are no celebrations after it, just a time to clean up. People eat and leave and not long after it started it is all done. We had the champagne fountain and a number of toasts given but apart from that there was no other type of formality. Thuy and I would go to every table and share a toast and then move on to the next. This was a little difficult for me as I don't touch alcohol but I did not want to be seen as turning my nose down at anyone, so I would have a little sip at each table and people were generally very understanding. Although only little sips I did feel the warmth of the rice wine as there were a lot of tables. We did not have a honeymoon as we would soon go to Australia to introduce Thuy to all of my family and that would suffice.

So now that I am married, I can go back to the story of my Aussie angel, Justine. Justine arrived in Ba Vi to volunteer with us for one month after which she was to go to central Vietnam to work in a monkey sanctuary. We were sad when she left as she was a very special human being and one that immediately showed a great love and concern for the kids. She had worked with the kids in Rooms 3 and 4 which are the two hardest rooms in the centre due to the severity of the disabilities. Justine looked past those disabilities and simply saw a group of kids in need of care.

Not too long after she had left I received a message from her that she apparently did not have the correct paperwork required by the government to do her other assignment at the sanctuary and asking if she could return to us. I had no hesitation in welcoming her back as people like her are a rare commodity. And so it was that almost eight years later she was still with us and acted as our Ba Vi coordinator. It had been difficult to find another coordinator in the village, firstly with enough English to interact with the volunteers, and secondly with enough time to actually be available for volunteers when needed. Justine was the first foreigner to work for RLF and will be the last. Justine moved back to Australia during COVID and again worked with children with disabilities and then went off for the past year travelling and seeing what the world had to offer.

It was time to continue building our HHV program, filling the gaps and giving the kids something to look forward to each day. Hien, a qualified teacher, was to be our next employee and we set up a classroom for her. But being an HHV worker is not just about carrying out a specific duty, it also means being prepared to help out with things like feeding time and assisting others in their programs when required. Hien taught Vietnamese and maths, and during her time with us has elevated six children to the level required to attend the local school. She also has another two students who could now attend school but both are confined to wheelchairs and unfortunately the school has no disability access and the centre will not commit to taking them to and from school. We had considered finding a way to get them there and providing the school with the access required but we are temporary here.

I would like to think that our involvement here will have no end but we are here at the mercy of the government and we don't really know what the future holds. If we were to find the funds to get them to school but later have to leave, their time at school would be over and we don't want another two broken-hearted children—they have had enough of that in their short lives. Hien also works with a variety of kids with slight intellectual disabilities and with hearing impairments; she is truly a patient, caring and loving woman. Needless to say, if we didn't provide an education for the kids at the centre they would have none at all and that should not be. It is the basic right of every child no matter where they live to have access to an education.

During our time here we have seen too many children leave us when they have had enough and are too tired to go on. It is so difficult for them here and I always have mixed emotions when one of them passes—sadness that their time has come but also in some ways grateful that they will finally be at rest and find peace. Although we use those terms 'at rest' and 'at peace', I am unsure if this is the case and won't really know until my time comes; I guess it is something we choose to believe and I certainly hope it is true as most of these little ones have suffered enough. If the Buddhist line of thought is to be followed, they will return in a far better form. Two of those children who passed on affected me a little more than most as I was quite close to them both. I had no more love for them than I do for all of the children here but sometimes certain people leave a footprint in your heart.

Duong and Thuy Van came to us with hydrocephalus, commonly referred to as water on the brain, and would both leave us a short time later. There are quite a number of these kids whose parents have them with them for as long as they can and then they are placed here for their final days. There is no cure for this disease but there are two types of operations that can be performed, one using a shunt and another procedure called endoscopic third ventriculostomy (ETV). Neither operation is a permanent cure and both are very dangerous operations. So even if we could fund the surgery, this is not the right place where a child can rehabilitate and we also have no control over such matters; we just do our best to care for them until their time comes.

Thuy Van spent the last of her time in the nursery and I became very close to her. She gave out an innocence that you couldn't help but feel and to me she glowed as if surrounded by a spiritual energy force. There was something special about this little one that drew me close. I think it was more of a spiritual connection, for although I knew what was going to happen in the near future, she always gave me a feeling of peace and when I held her nothing else really mattered. She was a beautiful young child and it was sad to know that her life would be so short; to me she was the epitome of what innocence and peace represented. I got that phone call one day when I was in Hanoi; more than a few tears rolled down my cheeks but again I hoped that she would be in a better place and my not wanting her to go was just a selfish act.

Duong was the other young one who also touched us all, more for his fighting spirit than anything else, and that one moment when he smiled. Duong's head was so much heavier than his little body and because the water was putting so much pressure on his brain, we thought he would only be with us for a very short time. But he battled on as if he didn't want to leave and he ended up with us for almost a year. There was a volunteer who before leaving had bought a beautiful burial gown for him but that too would have to wait to be worn.

I can only speak for myself and for other staff that I have asked but I never saw any type of emotion from Duong except to occasionally cry, which was totally understandable. He was nursed by volunteers or our staff but most times he would just lay with a blank expression on his face until one day when Phong, who was another resident of the centre and HHV worker (pictured below feeding Duong), sat across his chest in the cot and started playing with him and making silly noises, as you do. We were very lucky that someone was actually videoing this happening and for just a brief instant, Duong smiled; it didn't last long and it didn't happen again, but this day, it did. I was so happy when I saw the video as it wasn't too long after that time that he left us. It was just so satisfying for me to know that if this was truly the only time he smiled, he would move on knowing the emotion of happiness and also knowing that he was loved.

Phong feeding Duong

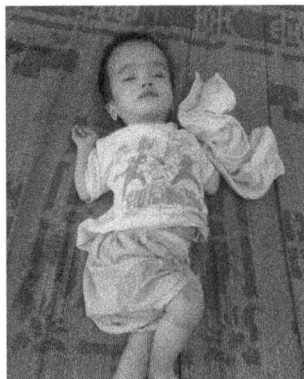

Thuy Van

Hanh was the Hanoi coordinator and used to meet with volunteers on arrival, conduct an orientation, show them the inner city and basically try to ensure they were comfortable before arranging their transfer to the Ba Vi centre. When it was time for her to leave she was replaced by another young woman called Luan. I first met Luan some time before at another disability program in Hanoi, when both she and her friend Hoai were graduating university but still found time to go out to the program and volunteer during any spare time they had. All RLF and HHV employees have a volunteering background and knowing that made it much easier for me to know we were getting the right personnel. Luan stayed with me for almost two years but left to have a baby, and it just so happened that at the time she left, Hoai was returning from a year travelling and working as a crop picker in New Zealand. Hoai has been with me for nearly four years and is now the manager of the RLF service and has taken over most of the administration duties.

It was always a dream of mine to have a soft room for the kids and another where they could express themselves artistically. So, along with some friends, I arranged another fundraiser and built a soft room and a creative therapy room, and with those rooms came two more employees.

The creative therapy room was originally run by Muoi, who was a brilliant teacher for the children, but unfortunately after approximately one year I didn't have the funds to keep her on and I had to let her go. Muoi could not work for nothing but I was very lucky to meet someone whose situation was a little different at the time, and she could. Her name is Phuong, she is a qualified teacher and she took over and managed the program. With help from volunteers she continued the great work that Muoi had started and has grown the range of activities for the kids. Our kids go there to express themselves, sometimes with art, sometimes with music; they may not win any prizes for either skill but they do have a good time and benefit greatly in an emotional sense from the sensory work and varied activities. Within a few months of her working voluntarily for us I found a sponsor for Phuong and she has now been an HHV employee for over four years.

My soft room also materialised and I love to go there and see the kids enjoying the room. I always envisioned it as a room for self-rehabilitation for the kids who had barely any movement in their bodies; if they could crawl or just drag themselves along, the soft room would be a great place for them. The colours of the room would give them mental stimulation and by trying as best they could to move around in a very safe environment, it would also serve to develop their core muscles. It did not take a great number of staff or volunteers to run the soft room as we would have no more than three kids in there at a time and someone only needed to sit and watch them, and give a little assistance when required.

Creative therapy room

Soft room

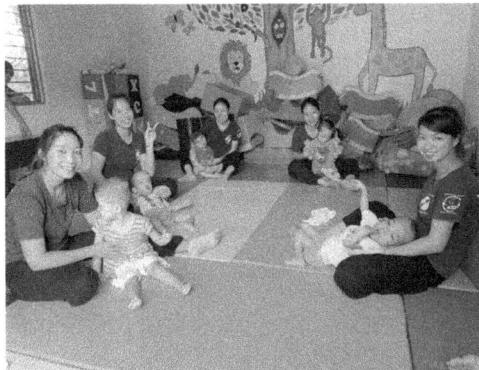

The role of an occupational therapist in its most simplistic form is to prepare children or adults to develop and maintain skills that they will need for independent living, normal day-to-day activities and also to design a program based on each person's individual disabilities that will allow them to achieve those goals. We were attracting a number of occupational therapists and university students who designed programs for the kids and worked with them during their time with us, but it soon became obvious that we needed a therapist of our own or the kids would derive no real benefit due to the inconsistency of practice.

Thuong, who lived at a nearby Buddhist pagoda, was our RLF Ba Vi coordinator at the time, having inherited that job from Ngan who, due to having a baby and family commitments, could not afford the time needed to fulfil the role. Thuong became our first occupational therapist worker and, like all others, developed her program with the help of the specialists that came our way. Also at this time, Justine assumed Thuong's role of Ba Vi coordinator. Like many before her, Thuong would find the man of her dreams and leave to start a family back in her hometown. This opened the door for Thuan, a friend of Thuong's, who also lived at the pagoda and was a trained nurse. She became our occupational therapist worker until a work opportunity in Hanoi arose and she was replaced by the wonderful Loan. It is always a little sad when losing any staff member but here it seemed that we would always replace them with someone equally as good. Only one more would leave before we had our current team intact and that was Been, who was another casualty of a lack of funding, but I am happy to say that she is now married and has a baby to occupy her time.

That Buddhist pagoda where Thuong and Thuan lived for a time also played a big part in cultural understanding for our volunteers, as each Wednesday we would go there for a vegetarian lunch provided by Su Co (the name given to a Buddhist nun; a Buddhist monk is referred to as 'Thay'). Our HHV program has helped many in the villages over the years through our relationship with Su Co, and we have also had volunteers go and stay at the pagoda on weekends for a better understanding of Buddhist teachings.

Thuy has been at my side through all of this and over the years has devoted her time to whatever needed to be done at the centre and whatever position needed to be filled for a day or two. Thuy is also my guide between East and West, not only with the centre staff and hierarchy, but also with our own staff. No matter how long you live here if you are not born and raised here and do not understand the life that most people have endured, you cannot pretend you know. It is not only a communist country but also predominantly a Buddhist country, with many traditions attached. I have lived here almost twelve years but still don't fully comprehend it all and would never claim to.

Thuy would guide me and I would teach her about management practices, again practised in a different way to her understanding, as my way has always been inclusive, to allow people to grow and take ownership of their own programs; to try to develop a worker who can take the skills they learn and move onto something better. I always saw myself more as a guide, someone for people to come to when advice or a decision that they have struggled with was needed. Although we always initially agreed the parameters of a particular job, I would always allow people to run and develop their programs to the best of their ability and only step in if I thought they were in danger of losing their way. Again, a little different here because again we are back in another time, the time of the big boss and the worker, but still, with a mixture of both cultures and styles Thuy this year became the manager of all our HHV programs and the volunteer service.

When working with staff I always remember a Richard Branson quote:

Train people well enough so they can leave, treat them well enough so they don't want to.
Richard Branson

Take care of your employees, and they will take care of your business. It's that simple.

Tham, who originally spent some time working in our rehab room and who is now our Rooms 3 and 4 activity coordinator, may provide some understanding through her own experience as to how some of these kids we have here actually end up in the centre. She married and lived in another small village some ten kilometres from the centre, and gave birth to a daughter called Linh. Not too long after her birth Linh developed a fever and almost lost her life and although she escaped with her life, the fever had a catastrophic effect on her brain, leaving her both intellectually and physically disabled.

Tham, like most others in her village, came from a very poor family and after the incident with Linh her husband left her, leaving her to provide for the family and care for Linh on her own. This was an impossible task in her small village, so Tham, forced into possibly the most difficult decision of her life, placed Linh in the centre and went to Hanoi to take a cleaning job to support the family. She is one of the most kind-hearted souls anybody could ever meet and despite her own personal difficulties, when she was not working in Hanoi she would volunteer in hospitals there.

Whenever she had a two-day break she would return to the family and spend as much time as she could with Linh at the centre, where I met her one day. I needed someone at the centre and it was not a difficult decision to employ Tham as she was loved by all; for me it was an opportunity to provide the means for her to see Linh every day. Later, Tham took Linh out of the centre and today with the help of her mum she cares for her at home.

Tham fell pregnant again and had another daughter; this time her child, Nhu y, was born with Down Syndrome. Tham had fallen pregnant as she was concerned about who would care for Linh when her own time comes and she had hoped to have a son. Nhu y is a wonderful young girl but it is very doubtful that she will ever be able to fill that role. Tham cannot afford to look that far ahead as she now has to work and care for them both at home with the same love and compassion she shows for all the kids at the centre.

Hoai and Thuy spend most of their weekdays at the centre when not greeting volunteers in Hanoi, with Hoai working in Room 5 and Thuy primarily in Room 7. I had covered most of the centre and had staff in almost every room so I was feeling happy that none would miss out on our service but there was still one more room to care for, and that was Room 6. It was a difficult room, not only because of the kids' behaviours, but also the centre staff's initial resistance to volunteers working in that room. I eventually found the funds and the right person to fill the role of activity coordinator with this group of kids and I also paid a small stipend to two resident members to personally care for two of the kids with behaviour that would always see them in trouble or locked in a room by themselves.

The residents we selected were obviously quite well adjusted and mature, and they would ensure that these kids got into no further trouble, due to their caring nature and their 24/7 supervision. They treated both as family—as a son for one and a small brother to the other. The person who we found for Room 6 was Loan, a good-natured young woman with an outgoing personality and a caring nature; she went on to establish a beautiful relationship with the kids and also gained the respect of the centre staff. She is assisted in the room by another of our resident staff named Giang, who has worked for us for four years now. As well as assisting Loan, she arranges our dance day every Thursday afternoon and teaches dance too.

Dance day is a special day when we take half of the kids to an old hall on site and dance the afternoon away. The kids always sense when it is their day for dancing and there is definitely a different vibe when it arrives. We take all of the kids that we can, whether they are mobile or not—they will arrive in wheelchairs, special support chairs and any form of transport necessary. For those who can dance, they do and for those in the chairs that cannot, they just enjoy the music from their chairs and move as best they can. For all who attend it is a very happy afternoon with both visual and mental stimulation; for our staff and me it is also a great time for us to bond as we all like to dance.

There was still one more hole to fill before I knew that this part of my vision would be complete. Before that happened I was to meet and begin working with another wonderful group of people at the House of Love—*Huong La*. That is a very appropriate name for this centre and I found it quite by accident one weekend when Thuy and I were coming back from a short break in Halong City.

Huong La

We had planned to spend the night in Bac Ninh city on our way back to Hanoi and we came across a friend who mentioned the centre; she seemed to think the centre could use some help so we made a call and arranged a visit for the following week. To my surprise, we met with a Catholic nun and found out that the centre was run by the Sisters of Unity, which had over a hundred nuns in the diocese of Bac Ninh province, but only twelve of them worked at the centre caring for over thirty children with varying degrees of disability.

This centre was far different from the Ba Vi centre in virtually every way. The sisters absolutely love the children and care for them in the best way they know possible. Among their group they have a nurse, though with limited knowledge of kids with disabilities and the best methods to care for them; but they did try and their results were very encouraging. The children here are all very clean and are bathed at least once and sometimes twice a day, their teeth are cleaned after every meal and they are, for the most part, a group of very happy kids.

The majority of the kids were placed at the centre because families or single mums were unable to properly care for them for a number of reasons, but each Lunar New Year holidays all but three are picked up and taken home to celebrate with family, sometimes for up to a month. It was also very easy to see during the visit that they did need help, especially with some of the kids with more severe disabilities. They were usually seated in some old children's car seats on top of chairs designed for people with disabilities that they would use to go to the toilet. It was also clear that all of the kids lacked activities and needed some programs that would stimulate their minds.

They spent most of their time in one big common room or, in mild weather they would go and play in an outdoor area; they had freedom and people who valued and loved them and that to me is always the most important part—everything else we can work on. Some of the older teenagers help the sisters make candles to provide income for the centre. There is nothing forced about this labour as the children willingly help as they do with other tasks, such as cleaning and feeding the more disabled kids. Everybody knows their tasks and they go about it for the most part with a smile on their face.

The first thing I knew we needed to do was to get to know each other a little better and to develop trust, so having seen what they do, we arranged a trip for them to Ba Vi. Em Hai, the head sister, and two of the younger sisters met Thuy and I at our place for breakfast one morning, after which we took them to Ba Vi to meet our team and to view our work.

They were excited when they arrived at Ba Vi because they knew they needed help and they wanted to see what we had in place and how we could apply some of our programs to Huong La. They were a little taken aback by the conditions the Ba Vi kids lived in but they are Vietnamese and have a greater understanding of the workings of the government than I will ever have so while not liking the environment, they did understand why it is as it is. They loved the programs that we had in place and light-heartedly asked if they could steal a couple of our workers.

From my time at their centre I knew one of the first things I needed to do was to take a couple of our specialists from Ba Vi to their centre to assess the kids with the more severe physical disabilities and put a rehabilitation schedule in place. This was something they had tried to do but at that stage had not been able to implement effectively. Em Hai took a great liking to the soft room and really wanted to see that happen at Huong La. They had a great day and asked a lot of questions and it was gratifying for me to bring the two groups together and to know that we were building a sustainable partnership and adding to our respective families.

Two weeks later I took Katie and Ellen, a volunteer physiotherapist, to Huong La for a few days to do a thorough assessment of the twelve kids we determined had the greatest needs. After the assessments, they conducted a half-day training session with the sisters on rehabilitation techniques they could use for each individual child. Through the efforts of Patty, an annual volunteer returnee with us, and with a little money from me, we had enough funds to purchase some much-needed equipment. We bought some special support chairs and wheelchairs, and Em Hai would see her soft room dream realised.

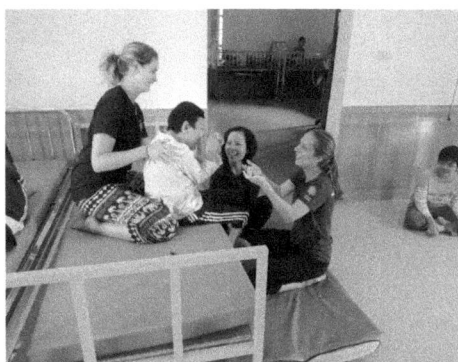

Huong La

I have volunteered there since our first meeting, usually alone but sometimes with Thuy and Hoai, and will continue to do so each week or until we can provide an HHV worker there so the kids can have the consistency of programs they need. The sisters converted a small house on the property and there I teach a little English to seven of the kids and make use of our new creative therapy room with many of the others. We have purchased some sporting equipment so that the kids can have some outdoor activities, and we have also started a nutrition program. The sisters grow all of the fruit and vegetables that they and the children eat so the nutrition program is to purchase protein for the kids as that will aid in their growth. There are ten kids at the centre who, due to their conditions, can only eat chao (rice porridge with a little strained vegetable).

I think creative therapy is so important for these kids as a means of expressing themselves in one of the art forms and also to feel included. What they create will have special meaning for them and you can see their joy when they know that they have created something special. It will always tell a story of the places they would like to be, the family they would like to have or the hurt they are feeling. Give a child some coloured pencils or paints and a piece of art paper and they create their world. It's amazing how many of them if given a pencil and asked to draw anything will most likely draw a small house with stick figures; some add a garden, trees or clouds in the sky.

I never look at their art and see nothing, and you don't need to be a psychologist to see either the happiness they desire or the hurt and frustration they are feeling. Usually their daily actions and their demeanour will duplicate their art. You cannot look at one of these kids and see just a child with bad behaviours, there is always a reason, as there is for people in your life; dig a little deeper and try to treat them accordingly. Nobody should be excluded; that is something that I would also address at Ba Vi with a new program.

I love the peace Huong La brings me through the warmth of the sisters and children; our meeting came along at a good time for both them and me—change was needed.

Twelve years is a long time to set up and be part of a highly charged emotional program such as Ba Vi and I needed to heed the warning signs, both physical and mental. As has happened so often in the past something came along that gave me that boost I required. This program has all of the ingredients needed to recharge my batteries and to move forward: peace, love, understanding and some wonderful caring people and children to surround myself with.

The sisters have no phones or internet to keep them informed of what is happening in the wider world. One day at lunch I asked if they had any idea of what was happening in the outside world; their reply was just one word: no. I thought, what a lucky group of people. It's wonderful to watch as they go about their work, their meditation and their prayers every day with a blissful smile on their faces, with no concern at all about what is happening in the outside world. I rarely view news from outside as nowadays it is mostly quite depressing so I just concentrate on the world before me as it presents itself.

Unfortunately, even Huong La is not immune to death and over the recent Lunar New Year we lost two young teenagers: Thuy, who passed while at home with her family for TET, and Thom, who passed shortly upon returning to the centre after the holiday. If there is any good to be found in death, I guess it could be that Thuy was with family when her time came and Thom passed peacefully.

I was actually at the centre when Thom passed and it was a shock for me, for although I have attended many funerals throughout my life and lost many at the Thuy An centre I had never actually viewed a dead person. It is my belief that the spirit moves on when we lose the life force and I personally would prefer to carry memories of the times we spent together, not of the lifeless body.

Thom had just returned after TET and was feeling tired so the sisters put him to bed to rest; he slept and didn't wake up again. They called me and told me what had happened; we went and viewed the body and then I assisted them with preparing Thom for his family to view as they fortunately only lived around twenty kilometres from the centre. It was all a little surreal to me as we moved and prepared both Thom and a private room for a service that the family members and friends would attend. A local priest was called in to conduct the service. Many tears were shed by all but then it was done and he had moved on to the great unknown, hopefully to find peace and to release the pain that he had felt for most of his young life.

As with all in my life that have passed, I do shed a tear, but no, I do not mourn them; when the moment comes I live with the wonderful memories we shared. Let them go and you let their spirit soar.

Death is never far away and we would be naive to think it won't strike us or those close to us at any time. People have different ways of enjoying their lives and different streams of thought on what that means. I am fortunate that I have made it this far and I now live each day as though it may be the last; not in celebration but going through each day in good conduct, smiling a lot, still trying to help at least one other person every day and valuing the relationships I have.

It's a simple philosophy but I know that if I was to go tomorrow, I will have no regrets as I will have had a fulfilled day the day before. So, if you think 'live like there is no tomorrow' means to go out and get drunk, take drugs and party, you are so wrong and I would urge you to rethink your way of life and your concept of what happiness is. Eat a meal with family and friends and put the phone aside; discover each other, do activities with them that do not involve technology or alcohol. If I could duplicate the days spent fishing with my family or the day the snow came to Gunnedah and we sat around the fire eating toast, talking and laughing, I would—that is living a quality life.

I now share almost every day with Thuy and we often ask each other where our happiness comes from; it seems a little unnatural to be so happy with no conflict. I guess our natures have aligned; we laugh and simply enjoy each other's company and with that we also have respect and love and a true commitment to enjoy each day we have together.

Final Pieces

Back at Ba Vi there was still one more piece to be put in place to complete the puzzle. We have a group of young teenage boys with either physical or intellectual disabilities, most of whom have lived in the rooms here for the better part of their lives. These young teenagers at the centre are either discovering their own sexuality or are violently acting out their frustrations because of their lives at the centre. Some act highly inappropriately in a sexually exploratory manner (something about which they are not educated and don't fully understand) or with violence against the fellow kids in the room.

They have no schooling on the ways of life and how to cope with their intellectual disability. It is debatable if they know right from wrong although their actions and the discipline that follows would make them aware that what they have done was not right. They are young teenagers growing up and have the same urges that most young boys do, but it is wrong on all levels that they would act out on those feelings in the way they do. The violence again comes from frustration, and the more they react the more they are disciplined and the more they inevitably react against that—an endless cycle, and the victims are sadly the other kids in the rooms.

Some of the centre staff have confided that they are too scared to discipline some of these kids, as they are quite strong and may react violently against them. The centre has no way to isolate these kids but to move them from the children's rooms to The Block with the older residents; unfortunately, at times they now become the victims as older and stronger people also act out their frustrations on them.

We work as a priority in the children's rooms and occasionally on The Block when needed. When these young teenage kids are placed on The Block they have a certain amount of freedom to walk around the centre and they will inevitably end up outside one of the rooms that we are working in, interfering with our activities and generally making a nuisance of themselves, causing friction between the centre staff, our HHV staff and them. They are truly isolated and if nothing is done, we will not only have a group of young children with bad behaviours, we will, in time, have a group of young men with bad behaviours; these kids are the forgotten ones.

As the monk said, it is the troubled ones that need our help the most; don't cast them aside, reach out.

I knew that we had to help them and I understood as best I could why they acted the way they did when they were in the rooms with the younger children and also the frustrations they felt based upon their current living conditions. They were really affecting everyone; they would continually act out, even vandalising our disability equipment and taking joy rides on our wheelchairs at lunchtime when everybody was resting. The only thing everyone at the centre was feeling towards them was anger. I wanted them to feel accepted and to know that somebody cared, and I wanted them to feel part of the community that is the centre. It may seem disjointed at times but it is its own little community and like other communities, it will have its ups and downs, its good and bad events.

When we are part of that wider community we need to act with understanding and respect for others, something they needed to learn; not through continual discipline but through feeling valued. If you have no love in your life but can feel just a little coming your way, it can have a very positive impact. I hoped we would reverse their feeling of isolation and defuse their frustrations, and rather than see them act out, see them help others. We also had young ones still in the rooms who, if we were not careful, would end up in the same situations as these boys; they would also be included so as to arrest their behaviours before they too found themselves in deep trouble.

My immediate thoughts were that the program should contain sports for they all had a liking for physical activity, but we would not include football as that could at times become very physical, and we wanted them working together not at each other's throats. We started with badminton, some ball games, aerobics, yoga and I also wanted dance as a means of relaxing and for pure enjoyment. My ultimate goal is to see the group dance at the international disability day celebrations in Hanoi, and over time assess the skills of each and possibly see one or more of them compete in the South East Asian Special Olympics.

This would take time but now we had a goal and we just needed to work towards it. I had seen some resident friends from the Quynh Hoa centre compete for Vietnam at the South East Asian Special Olympics and also other members of their group perform dance at the Vietnam Disability Day celebrations. It may be a little harder for our centre but most things are possible if you believe. Setting goals too high can lead to disappointment and as I was not the one that would be hurt if things didn't work out, it was important that we were also realistic in what we could achieve; let's first just plant it, then nurture it and watch it grow.

I left the recruitment of the program coordinator to Thuy, Hoai and Hien, who together interviewed ten locals and through the process found a wonderful young woman named Trang to fill the position. I also found a sponsor from the USA for a one-year trial through some good friends and ex-volunteers, Luke and Donna, who also fundraise for our medical program. Trang runs yoga and aerobic classes from her home at night and is very sporty and, like all in Vietnam, she loves to dance. At the time of writing Trang has only been running the program for a few months but already the results are promising. The boys now have something meaningful in their lives and every day they enjoy the program activities. Now, instead of coming to our work areas to annoy us, they are coming to help out and to interact with us and the other kids. It will have its ups and downs but I am sure it will have a meaningful impact on all at the centre over a longer period of time.

I have confidence that the centre will have continual improvement. Recently a lot of external work was carried out to give the centre more open spaces and at the same time a more homely feeling. The kids without intellectual disabilities as they grow older are now helping out with those that do, and overall you feel a sense of moving forward. It will take time and we need patience, but as our working relationships continue to grow with the government staff from the centre so do the benefits for the kids.

Red Lotus may be gone but it is absolutely vital for the continued physical and emotional growth and wellbeing of the kids here that Helping Hands Vietnam continues. If we can retain the wonderful support that we get from people like Luke and Donna from America who fundraise every year for the medical program, alongside The Presbyterian Ladies College in Sydney, Australia who are led by the wonderful Issy and fundraise for our general program, then I am sure it will. Thank you also to people like Tony and Andrew who sponsored an individual worker each for many years, to others that help when they can and to those that will in the future.

Hoai

Thuy

Hien

Tam Anh

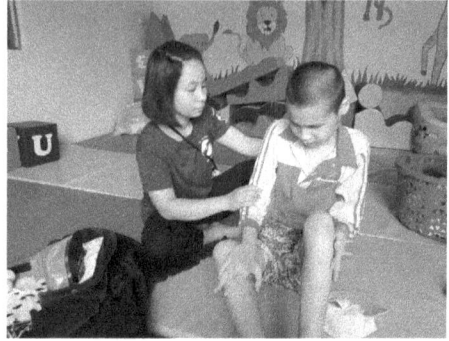

Phuong

Nang

Justine

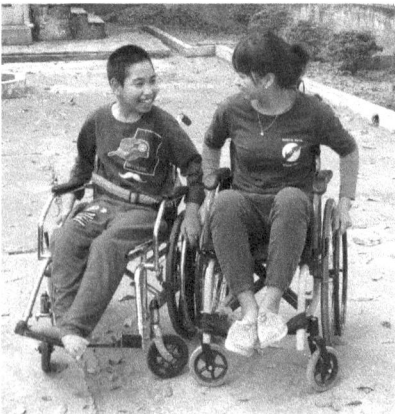

Thuan

Katie

Carly

Chuyen

Trang

Tham

Loan

Current Red Lotus Foundation and Helping Hands Vietnam staff

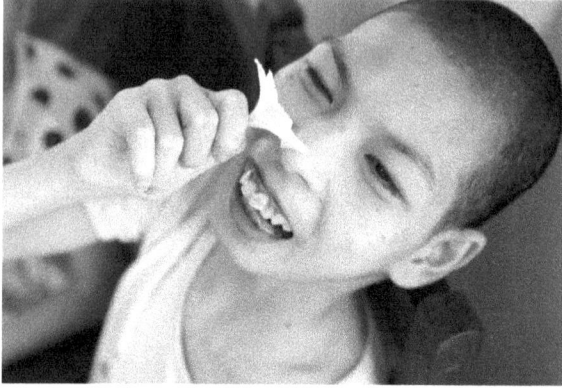

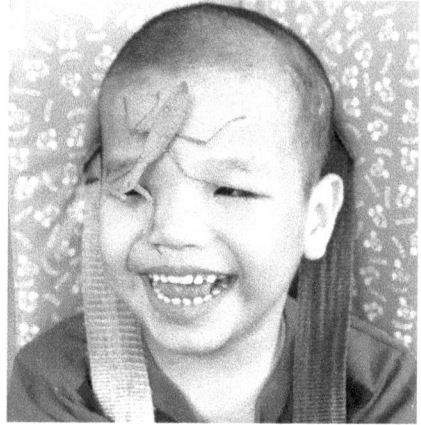

Our Daily Goal – Smiles

Now

The world is full of good people. If you can't find one, be one.
Mother Teresa

I am a lucky man. My world is full of good people—the kids I work with, the special people who work with me, the Sisters of Unity, the friends I have and of course, my family. Very early in life I decided that if people were to remember me at all it should be simply as 'he was a good man'. Nothing grand, just something simple but philosophical enough to tell my story. For me, that was all that I could strive for; I have no desire to be rich and famous, I just like to contribute in a small way to those I can help and to live my life in good conduct. I don't know that I am worthy of those few words yet, that is for others to decide. I just try each day to work towards them.

I don't see good or bad people. I do see bad things happening in this world but with people I believe it is both environmental and circumstantial that some receive the 'bad person' tag. We are all a result of the environment we grow up in and the circumstances that surround us in that time of growth from childhood to adulthood. We eventually make our own decisions but they are often made within the boundaries of the societies in which we live, or those we find difficult to live in.

Social media plays a major role now in the conditioning of human beings. The number of both young and older people committing suicide is at a level never seen before in this world and those numbers continue to grow, as do rates of depression. Young people I have known or do know trying to take their own lives,

193

some unfortunately succeeding, simply because of the pressure being applied by our own, at times, unrealistic standards.

When are you good enough?

I have nothing of a material nature and I am not sure what lies ahead for me as I age further; I will just continue to flow and see what happens. I will address the things I can do and not let worry or the perceptions of society rule me. I will awake tomorrow to another day and address it when it comes as best I can. I am happy, and that is all that really matters. The things people worry about may never come, or we may not be here to see them come. So I only have the here and now, short-term plans for the morrow. What will be, will be—only I can change that with the choices I make and those choices will be made when the time arrives, not infinite times in my head today.

I have the rest of my life to look forward to and even at my advanced age I know that may be longer than many I know. I have even decided when that will be. It will occur when my little daughter Ula turns 21 years of age and I will pass peacefully. If you believe in it strong enough it will occur. I have been to a doctor once in the past eleven years, I had a small kidney stone that I passed using natural meds. Now I just drink a lot of water ⏣ Stress kills, I have no time for it.

Tomorrow is Thuy's birthday and we will spend a little time together and then she will go with her Buddhist group to a pagoda to celebrate both Buddha's and her birthday. For me, I don't know yet. I will await the day and then embrace it as it comes. I do know something for certain—I will enjoy it.

It's not important who I am
It is important what I do, and the manner in which I do it
Zet

Who is Ula?

After seven years of trying and seven IVF attempts we received a wonderful present for the Xmas of 2021. Our little daughter Ula joined us and completed our little family. Thuy became a mum for the first time and I a dad for the fifth time. The doctor said that Buddha must be shining on us and I believe he is.

As she was born a Vietnamese national it was quite acceptable to use my surname on her birth certificate but she had to have a

Vietnamese first name, so her official name is Tue Linh (meaning intelligent/smart) and that she is. Her house name and more generally used name is Ula (meaning precious/rare) as that is who she was always going to be.

Who is Kya?

Another surprise. We still had one swimmer in the IVF bank and Thuy continued to pay for its storage. I didn't really mind as it would be good if it actually worked for Ula to have a sibling and we both agreed if it did not happen then that would be it, we would try no more. It did happen and Ula will have a little sister Kya (meaning Diamond in the Sky) at around the same time as Ula's 2nd birthday.

What lies ahead for these little ones, who knows? We will play our part as their guides in their initial years and eventually they will make their own decisions.

Ula

(Tue Linh Donnelly)

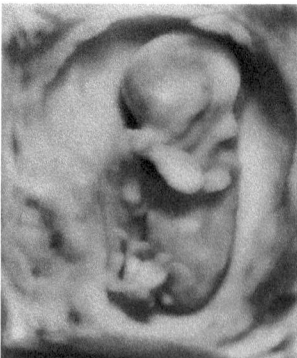

Kya

Just a few of the wonderful friends and family from the world over who have made this part of my journey so memorable – Much Love – Thank you

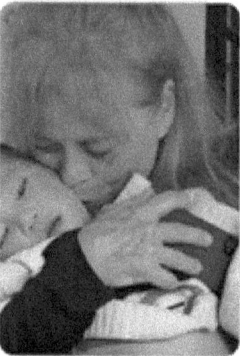

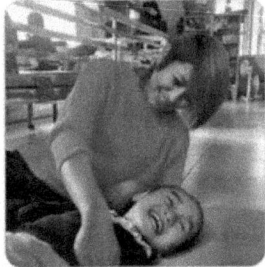

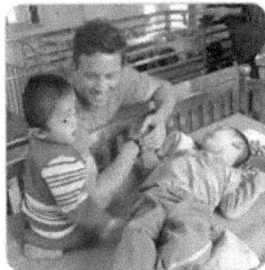

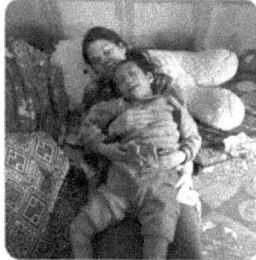

A Parable

It has many different interpretations—none right, none wrong. What are your thoughts?

A man travelling across a field encountered a tiger.

He fled, the tiger after him.

Coming to a precipice, he caught hold of the root of a wild vine and swung himself down over the edge.

The tiger sniffed at him from above.

Trembling, the man looked down to where, far below, another tiger was waiting to eat him.

Only the vine sustained him.

Two mice, one white and one black, little by little started to gnaw away the vine. The man saw a luscious strawberry near him. Grasping the vine with one hand, he plucked the strawberry with the other.

How sweet it tasted!

Zen Flesh—Zen Bones

www.ingramcontent.com/pod-product-compliance
Lightning Source LLC
Chambersburg PA
CBHW051208090426
42740CB00021B/3423